Ministry Leadership

Developing the Blueprint of Discipleship

Dr. Juanita Foster
Sr. Pastor Teresa S. McCurry

Copyright © 2021 by Dr. Juanita Foster

All rights reserved. This book or any portion thereof may not be reproduced or used in any manner whatsoever without the publisher's express written permission except for the use of brief quotations in a book review.

Printed in the United States of America

First Printing, March 8, 2021

ISBN Print:
ISBN: 978-1-7338770-4-6

Published by:
MCCURRY MINISTRIES INTERNATIONAL

Ministry Leadership

Contents

Introduction: Ministry Leadership 7

Chapter 1: Spiritual Responsibility 19

Chapter 2: Good Stewards of your Time 33

Chapter 3: Speak Life: Communicating Effectively 45

Chapter 4: Qualified Leaders to Assist you:
                Delegation Of Tasks 59

Chapter 5: Disagreement with your Brother/Sister 71

Chapter 6: My Brothers Keeper: Caring for others 83

Chapter 7: A threefold cord is not quickly broken. 101

Chapter 8: Self-Care and Stress Management: 119

Chapter 9: Conclusion 141

About the author 155

Ministry Leadership

A *man of God once* said "The Church is the most leadership-intensive organization in the world. Church leaders need to look in God's Word for leadership principles."

Why Leadership?

Leadership is a mechanism of social power that maximizes the efforts of others to achieve a goal. Leadership has little to do with seniority or a place in the hierarchy of a corporation. We don't need to exercise leadership with extroverted motivational qualities. Many with charisma may not lead automatically. Good management is required to schedule, calculate, track, organize, resolve, recruit, fire, and so many other things. Usually, administrators are handling things. Leaders are Visionaries and Managers, execute the vision.

How we define Christian leadership is the crucial starting point for teaching leadership. Christian leadership is a process of influencing a community to use their God-given gifts toward a goal. There are additional skills of leadership one can learn. Growing as disciples personally include developing as a leader specifically. At our Church New Beginning Ministries in Cleveland, Ohio, we have a Discipleship pairing. When new people join the ministry we pair them with a senior leader, minister, pastor or elder for Discipleship in the monthly meetings we are teaching biblical precepts, while modeling and guiding others toward living righteously as followers of Jesus Christ. Our Goal is for this to be a cyclical process—meaning once you are discipled, you are to disciple others, and so on. One of the most important characteristics of being a disciple (a student or pupil), is to develop an intimate relationship with God through Christ rather than just learning about Him. Discipleship equips the believer with God's Word, prayer, doctrine, worship, encouragement, and service. Discipleship training is also all about the relationship with others. Relationships are developed by sharing oneself, devotions, care, and encouraging each other toward living as believers in our everyday lives.

Very often, the best teachers share from experience and testimonies of how they overcame in their own journeys. Telling others believers what following Christ has done for you personally, can have an invaluable impact on those who are yearning, looking and searching for the same kind of transformation in their lives. This is absolutely necessary; an extremely important part of discipleship.

Christian leadership is not about the accumulation of power. It is about empowering others. Theologian John Stott said it best when he said: "authority by which the Christian leader leads is not power, but love. Not force, but for example, not coercion, but reasoned persuasion". Leadership is the capacity to translate vision into reality.

As a leader, it is very important for your team to know and understand your vision

Leadership is the act of influencing/serving others out of Christ's interests in their lives, so they accomplish God's purposes for and through them. Christian leadership is not rooted in worldly notions of success, such as the love of money or power. Jesus called his disciples to Himself and said, *"The Son of Man did not come to be served, but to serve, and to give His life a ransom for many" (Matthew 20:28).* The Bible also says Jesus spoke about this greatly when expressing the importance of serving others.

In today's society, the words "leadership" and "heart" are not generally included in the same phrase. Christian leaders are led by delicate bonds of love rather than tight control lines. It's not enough to love your children unconditionally; you have to love them in ways that express the love to them. Love is expressed by focused attention, eye contact and verbal encouragement says the poet. As individuals and believers in God's word, we need to create a loving relationship with ourselves to be able to love and lead ourselves. Then, we can help disciple others to achieve the same thing. As a leader, we must be first partakers.

Becoming a leader requires a great deal of love; you can't lead God's people if you do not love them. Because when you love someone, you have their best interests at heart, you want to see them grow. You want to see great and mighty things happen to them and around them. Love is the key ingredient that makes a Christian leader different from every other leader.

Self-development is something all Christian leaders should possess. Even Jesus was an advocate of self-development there were several times he would leave the crowd and go to a quiet place to meditate and edify his spirit by praying and speaking in tongues. As a Christian leader, you are like a model for your followers; they look up to you for almost everything. I have seen people who act and talk like their church leaders because they see characters they would like to emulate.

You see them copy the leader even down to the way he dresses. I am talking about the fact that the leader is the model for the people; leaders are encouraged to develop themselves every day - mentally, physically, spiritually and otherwise. Keep yourself under a current flow of God's anointing, and you'll see your flock also wanting to keep up with you. Paul puts it in a nice way when he said in 1 Corinthians 11:1 *"follow me as I follow Christ".*

Correcting others in the right way is essential for all Christians. Many passages in Scripture speak to this principle, as the following examples illustrate. Many pastors have concerns about engaging with members of the sinning community. Paul teaches Timothy how to perform the gentle art of rectification. Correction is never an easy activity, but a part of divine love. Churches and families appear to run down into the ditch without correction, Paul says. We all have relationships that sometimes require us to give biblical correction if we really love others. How can Christian leaders approach correcting others in the right way? The Bible offers the following tips: Don't be foolish and ignorant, knowing that they dispute. Be patient with all, and be gentle with those who are in opposition. The Bible also offers tips on dealing with unruly people, upholding the weak, and challenging their flaws.

If you know Christ, you are the Lord's bond-servant. As such, He will hold you accountable for being faithful to Him.

We are afraid that if we try to correct someone else, he (or she) will point the finger back at us. It is always more of a hassle to correct than to let it go. But, we are commanded to pursue love, which always requires effort and risk. It takes effort to arrange a time to get together to talk about such matters. You risk a backlash from the other person. You need to fear God more than you fear people. I Corinthians 14:1 *Follow the way of love and eagerly desire gifts of the Spirit, especially prophecy.*

Integrity: People don't follow leaders who lack integrity. Integrity involves actions as well as words. Now, I am not so much referring to things like not stealing as I am to hypocrisy. Integrity involves practising what we preach, being consistent and dependable, doing what we say we will do and living in such a way that others will trust us. **Integrity in leaders** refers to being honest, trustworthy, and reliable. Acting in accordance with your words by owning your mistakes, as opposed to hiding, blaming or making excuses.

In short, the Christian command of honesty is an order to both speak and act in the manner of Jesus. It is a life marked by love, compassion, mercy, justice, and upholding the call of God above all else. The Bible does not address integrity by name, but the word "honesty" is sometimes used in references to living a life of the highest integrity. It is also often used to characterize walking in the path of Faith and to prevent hypocrisy.

Passion: Rather than deceive or manipulate followers, good leaders inspire others. In Nehemiah 2:17, Nehemiah inspired the people fearlessly to restore Jerusalem's walls; He put forth a vision, expressed a plan, and told the people of God that God was with them. When we move people, we control and exploit them for our gain. But when we call people to a higher cause, we get them inspired.

In leadership literature, passion is often associated with what happens to leaders when they don't have it. In addition to your personality, natural talents and gifts, you need to understand and tap into your passions. Passions are like threads of inner concern that tightly form a rope strong enough to support your dreams when woven together. Passionate leaders are fully engaged in the process no matter what the process is and committed to achieving the goals and task at hand at the same time helping others achieve their objectives as well. When you're around a passionate leader, your sensory system is stimulated (your baby leaps, Luke 1:41-44), your emotions are shaken as you pick up their positive, infectious energy.

How Is Biblical Leadership Different From Worldly Leadership?

There are literally thousands of educational tools for leadership available today, from books, podcasts and blogs to personal coaching, seminars and workshops. But is all leadership education and training equal? Do all the methods and angles of teaching end up leading to the same place?

I think the response is a resounding "no" because they do not have the same end goal in mind. By analyzing the following three main points, the primary contradictions between biblical leadership and the leadership style the world provides can be seen.

Firstly, biblical leadership aims at the leader's heart. Every tactical issue within the leader can be traceable to how they are at heart. Before any other lasting personal and organizational change can occur, the heart of a leader must be transformed. World leadership tends to dismiss or undervalue the need for internal change.

According to a recent survey, less than 20 per cent of leaders have a strong sense of their own individual purpose. Traditional leadership resources focus on the "What" and the "How," but ignore the "Why". Jesus rejected fame, wealth, and earthly applause because He knew His intent. Once we understand why, we will be much more effective with what and how. "**Purpose is not what we do or even how we do it. Purpose is what distinguishes biblical leadership from the rest.**" It requires soul-searching, understanding one's core values of life, and a desire for a destination that is far more than just profit or personal success.

Secondly, Biblical leadership aims at bringing others into a closer relationship with Jesus. It does not use people as the means to achieve certain ends. Biblical leadership is built on love, grace, forgiveness and putting others before self. Don't be taken in by worldly "experts" that promise change and success apart from the biblical model that Jesus gives us. Only His way brings true change and lasting results. It recognizes that leaders are stewards (managers) entrusted by God with certain responsibilities. It acknowledges God to be the ultimate audience and authority over all things. It considers serving others, as the highest form of leadership as reflected in these words of Jesus: "You know that the rulers of the Gentiles lord over them." This is not so in Biblical leadership.

Why is it important to have leaders in our churches? In the Church, leadership is far more than just a term. It's about how the leaders communicate with the culture of the Church. It is difficult for a church, without the right leaders, to continue to survive for decades.

Finally, Church leadership is essential to direct the group through transformation successfully. One of the church leaders' most critical tasks is inspiring and empowering their members, workers. When a Member feels confused, leaders should listen to their concerns. It is not always an easy job, but it is one of a very successful church leader's characteristics.

The Church is not an activity solely for the weekend. It is the responsibility of church leaders to carry on with service all week long. To keep in touch with potential members, leaders need to consider new and existing trends, such as promoting the Church online, especially in this period when the world is under the grip of the deadly coronavirus.

Church should not be just something that's happening on Sundays. Strong leadership works with current members to create a more successful approach to attract new church guests. Without the right leadership, the church group does not get what it really wants, and that is the secret to retaining members and growing membership.

By far, the most significant justification for church leadership is to put together the whole church family as one. It is almost difficult to keep everyone involved and participating when members, employees and casual guests are not all on the same page. Instead, you see membership being random, members becoming unable to get along and more members questioning their own faith. It takes good leadership to put together so many different people. You have thousands of people from different backgrounds, even with a small ministry. It's not easy to get them all to meet less than one roof to share their faith. Successful leadership is what brings and holds a church together.

Who Is Qualified To Lead In The Church?

Knowing this answer would help us determine who was ready to lead now and in the future. We'd also have a framework for disciplining these potential leaders.

Is the person committed to Jesus? (1 Timothy 3:6- Not a novice, lest being lifted up with pride he falls into the condemnation of the devil, 1 Timothy 5:22, 1 Samuel 13:14)

Is the individual a fully-devoted follower of Christ? When picking a leader in the Church, it is important to at least check if the said individual is fully devoted to the ways of God and a true believer. You can't pick as a leader someone with shaky faith as their hearts can be easily corrupted by evil thoughts, and this will in turn, affect the hearts of the followers. Do they pursue Jesus passionately? Again the word love comes into play. When picking a leader, it must be someone who actually loves God and pursues the things of God.

Are they recent converts or have they had time to prove their faith is true? This part can be a bit tricky, but the truth is plain, a new convert cannot be put in place of leadership immediately.

This is because their faith is still new and developing; having them in leadership may be a bad decision as they will be faced with so many challenges that perplex even the most mature Christian minds. Again, they have to prove their faith. Most people can become indecisive, especially when faced with challenges. Having a new Christian in leadership may be a wrong move, especially when trials and temptations arise. They could immediately run back to their old ways.

Another characteristic that qualifies a person for a Christian leadership position is good character. Does the individual have a solid character? Do they possess self-control? Are they gentle, hospitable, upright, holy, and disciplined? The fruit of the spirit is the character of Christ.

> 1Timothy 3:1-7 Here is a trustworthy saying: If anyone sets his heart on being an overseer, he desires a noble task. Now the overseer must be above reproach, the husband of but one wife, temperate, self-controlled, respectable, hospitable, able to teach, Not given to drunkenness, not violent but gentle, not quarrelsome, not a lover of money. He must manage his own family well and see that his children obey him with proper respect. (If anyone does not know how to manage his own family, how can he take care of God's Church?) He must not be a recent convert, or he may become conceited and fall under the same judgment as to the devil. He must also have a good reputation with outsiders so that he will not fall into disgrace and into the devil's trap.

Are his or her actions reflective of someone who is entirely devoted to Christ? For example, is their marriage solid? Are they a good parent to their children? Do they have a quick temper?

Do they have a good comprehension of God's Word? Can the person identify false doctrine? Do they defend the Christian faith and encourage people to take steps in spiritual maturity?

> Colossians 1:28-29 He is the one we proclaim, admonishing and teaching everyone with all wisdom, so that we may present everyone fully mature in Christ. 29 To this end, I strenuously contend with all the energy Christ so powerfully works in me.

Is the individual considering this to be an appointment from God or from men? Is there a clear sense that this is God's calling? Is it God's will? Do they have a concern for helping lost people find Jesus? Does their heart beat fast when discussing ministry opportunities to reach people who haven't heard about Christ?

> Acts 20:28 Keep watch over yourselves and all the flock of which the Holy Spirit has made you overseers. Be shepherds of the Church of God,[a] which he bought with his own blood.

> 1 Peter 5:2 Be shepherds of God's flock that is under your care, watching over them—not because you must, but because you are willing, as God wants you to be; not pursuing dishonest gain, but eager to serve

---- CHAPTER 1 ----

Spiritual Responsibility

ACCOUNTABILITY
Responsibilities of Church Leaders
(Hebrews 13:7, 17-19, 22-25)

Ministry leaders are responsible to lead.
Ministry Leadership requires having a clear biblical picture of what the local church should be and what it ought to be doing and regularly communicating that to the Body of Believers. It also requires dealing with problems that arise in the church. Yes, the church has some problems.

The New Testament does not instruct a distinction between "clergy" and "the body," in that every believer is a priest with full access to God (1 Peter 2:9). *You are a chosen generation -* The titles formerly given to the whole Jewish Church, all who believed in Christ, whether Jews or Gentiles, and who received the baptism in the name of the Father, and of the Son, and of the Holy Ghost. They were also a royal priesthood, or what Moses calls a kingdom of priests, Exodus 19:6. For all were called to sacrifice to God, and he is represented to be the King of that people, and Father of those of whom he was king; therefore, they were all royal.

Leaders and followers in the local church are to be held accountable. The New Testament uses different names or titles to refer to church leaders. They are called elders (Acts 20:17), which refers to maturity in the faith. They are called overseers who are Elders within each congregation who work within a "body of elders", several of whom are assigned to oversee specific congregational tasks. Each body of elders has a Coordinator (different ministries have different titles for Overseer), a Secretary, and a Service Overseer. (1 Tim. 3:1, 2), which refers to their function of superintending the church. (In Titus 1:5, 7 and Acts 20:17, 28 the two terms are used of the same office). They are called pastors (Eph. 4:11), which means shepherds. Peter uses all three of these terms (1 Pet. 5:1, 2). Few passages show the importance of the "eldership" in the early church more clearly. It is to the elders that Peter specially writes and he, who was the chief of the apostles, does not hesitate to call himself a fellow-elder. It will be worth our while to look at something of the "eldership's" background and history, the most ancient and the most important office in the Church, when he exhorts the elders to *"shepherd [pastor] the flock of God among you, exercising oversight...."* He goes on (verse 4) to refer to Christ as "the Chief Shepherd" (or, Pastor).

Another word for church leaders is the Greek verb, *prohistemi*, (lit., "to stand before") which is translated "have charge over" (1 Thess. 5:12). It refers to the function of elders "who rule well" (1 Tim. 5:17). It also refers to a man's responsibility to "manage" his own household (1 Tim. 3:4, 5, 12).

Ministry leaders are responsible to walk personally with God.

In 1 Timothy 4:16, Paul exhorts his younger co-worker, *"Pay close attention to yourself and to your teaching…."* Paul's concluding verse in this passage offers much wisdom. First, Timothy is to evaluate himself. The areas he is to focus on are both his life and his teaching. Both were developed earlier in this chapter and are essential to effective ministry. The ability to understand, teach, and live out the truths of the gospel is essential to the work of a Ministry leader. Paul refers to persistence, a key theme both in physical training and in our spiritual life. For example, Hebrews 12:1 teaches, *"… let us run with endurance the race that is set before us."* Timothy's persistence would *"save both yourself and your hearers."* This was not about Timothy earning his salvation. He was saved by faith (Ephesians 2:8–9). However, he could save his life and those of his church from false teaching errors through his example and by teaching the truth.

In Acts 20:28, he told the Ephesian elders, *"Be on guard for yourselves and for all the flock…."* Our text brings out four aspects of the personal walk of church leaders:

1. MINISTRY LEADERS MUST MAINTAIN A GOOD CONSCIENCE BEFORE GOD AND OTHERS.

2. MINISTRY LEADERS LIVE WITH A VIEW OF ANSWERING TO GOD SOMEDAY.

3. MINISTRY LEADERS ARE MEN & WOMEN OF FAITH AND PRAYER, WHO ENCOURAGE OTHERS TO DO THE SAME.

4. MINISTRY LEADERS ARE WILLING TO SUFFER FOR CHRIST IF NEED BE.

5. MINISTRY LEADERS HAVE TO BE OPEN TO HEARING FROM THE HOLYSPIRIT.

Ministry leaders are responsible to work together.

"Leaders" is plural. The New Testament clearly teaches that the local church's leadership is to be plural (Acts 14:23; 20:17; Titus 1:5). Plural leadership is a safeguard against the abuse of authority. Also, the task of shepherding a local church is far too great for one man, unless the church is very small. There are two implications of this truth:

1. Paul tells the church to greet their leaders (13:24). It is the leaders (plural) who keep watch over the souls of the flock (13:17). Obviously, they could only do this by working together as a team.

2. The whole Bible is summed up by the two great commandments, which are both relational: Love God and love others. This means that Ministry leaders must work at relating to one another in love, and they must work at helping church members relate to one another in love.

> Ecclesiastes 4:9-12 Two people are better off than one, for they can help each other succeed. If one person falls, the other can reach out and help. But someone who falls alone is in real trouble. Likewise, two people lying close together can keep each other warm. But how can one be warm alone? A person standing alone can be attacked and defeated, but two can stand back-to-back and conquer. Three are even better, for a triple-braided cord is not easily broken.

Solomon in these verses speaks of the vanity, or emptiness, of a miser who remains alone, yet works tirelessly and continually. Two workers are better than one because they will produce more efficiently when they work together. A threefold cord is more than three times as strong as a single cord. The Lord can give us strength and blessings that we could never get on our own. In a God led relationship, where the Lord is called upon to lead and guard, there is a threefold Cord. It is vital for believers to make the Lord Head of their relationships and heads of their homes. The Bible says that if there is an accident while working, the one will be able to help the other, and if one is alone, one might get hurt, but there is no one to help him or get medical attention for him. If there's a cold night, two together will produce heat, helping to keep each other warm.

"Many are one" concept is behind the "many are together" concept, which is the key to church leadership. Each person must be convinced of their part in the whole of the Church will be weak. If church leaders don't have this concept well defined in their soul, they will act selfishly, independently and hurt each other, he says. Two are better than one, and God chooses to dwell in His people as one, he writes. *"If we hurt any, then we are defiling the whole temple of God where God dwells,"* he says in 1 Corinthians 3:16-17. *Don't you know that you yourselves are God's temple and that God's Spirit dwells in your midst? If anyone destroys God's temple, God will destroy that person; for God's temple is sacred, and you together are that temple.* When we work together for a common cause, valuing and treasuring those close to us, then what we do will flourish.

Ministry leaders are expected to be accountable

Accountability is the obligation to give a reckoning or explanation for one's actions. The goal is to help people grow in Christ and learn to find Him as the source, force and course of life. In the church setting managing the Church is an obligation to 'give a reckoning' or explanation. The Church's mandate is to carry out the Church's mission and to 'carry out its programs'. Accountability is not just a matter of checks and balances; it is about human relationships. Leaders should never serve without a support structure to maintain their focus and purity. Where there is an absence of accountability, there is often a culture of impunity, a disregard for norms, values and decency.

> Hebrews 4:13-16 (New International Version) [13]Nothing in all creation is hidden from God's sight. Everything is uncovered and lay bare before the eyes of him to whom we must give account. [14]Therefore since we have a great high priest who has ascended into heaven,[a] Jesus the Son of God, let us hold firmly to the faith we profess. [15]For we do not have a high priest who is unable to empathize with our weaknesses, but we have one who has been tempted in every way,

> just as we are—yet he did not sin. ¹⁶Let us then approach God's throne of grace with confidence, so that we may receive mercy and find grace to help us in our time of need.

Accountability is a tool for Personal change and strengthening performance. The definition of accountability is the processes through which an organization's processes are carried out. The Ministry's activities are not overshadowed by the interests of the most powerful members, and the concept of understanding of each group relates to the ability or otherwise of each group to bring about change within the Ministry. It is the Ministry leaders' responsibility to be accountable to each group - whether it is a regulatory, legal or contractual, financial or ethical responsibility, or just a group of people. It's the senior leadership's obligation to respond to the needs of the congregation and the ability of each of them to be representative of the ministry's vision.

In order for the organization to be considered truly accountable, they ought to answer two questions, are they preparing or repairing? Without a plan for your personal growth, you will be reacting to Life instead of living on purpose. You'll be forced to make repairs on your life because it will fall short of its potential. So, here is the question: Do you want to invest time preparing, or spend time repairing? Martha and Mary are vivid illustrations of these two drives or compulsions. Martha wants to impress Jesus, and she attempts to perform for Him. Mary determines she must be served by Jesus before she attempts to serve him.

> **Romans 14:12 – Yes, each of us will give a personal account to God.**

Paul wrote in Romans 3:23 that all of us have sinned and fallen short of God's glory. God will not respond to the account we give of ourselves and then decide if we deserve heaven or hell. Instead, we will give Christ an account of our works in this life, and they will be shown to be lasting or worthless. Believers will be rewarded for their lasting works and suffer a loss of some kind for their worthless ones. Everyone there, though, will stand in Christ and be saved. The decision about whether we will be allowed into heaven has already been made for those who are in Christ.

According to Paul; every person, Believers and non-Believers, is accountable before a sovereign God. Jesus emphatically taught that a day of judgment is coming when every person will have to give an account. Man is a rebel who wants to do his own thing without any or very little accountability for his actions. Without a sense of accountability, the world can quickly gravitate in the direction of the ruthless acts and tyranny of people like Hitler. When God either does not exist in men's beliefs or when the truth about God is disputing, the truth is disputable. The Bible says, *"As I live, says the Lord, every knee will bow to me, and every tongue will give praise to God" (Rom 14:10-12).*

According to the directives of Scripture, accountability to God and to one another is the foundation for freedom and liberty. Many see freedom as the right to abandon accountability to God to do what they please in the promotion of self-gratification. But that is not freedom. It is slavery or at least leads to slavery.

Beliefs or one's world view always has consequences. It's like a train which is free to do what it was created to do as long as it is on its track. Freedom is both the responsibility and the ability, by the grace of God, to do what is right according to righteous standards of truth.

Accountability is one of the means God uses to bring about solid growth and maturity with the freedom to be what God has created us for. The Bible, in no way, denies our individualism. Indeed, it promotes it, but in a way that holds us each accountable to others. You can't make disciples or produce growing and mature Believers without accountability.

> For we must all stand before Christ to be judged. We will each receive whatever we deserve for the good or evil we have done in this earthly body (2 Corinthians 5:10).

Paul insists that all believers in Jesus will appear before the judgment seat of Christ when He returns to earth. Christ will then declare at that moment whether someone will go to heaven or hell. Every good action will be rewarded. Christians will receive those efforts "back from the Lord". The works of those who have lived only for themselves will be "burned up" or shown to be worthless. God's grace to us in forgiving sin does not mean He's careless about how Christians live their earthly lives. It declares our time as spent well or foolishly, courageously or cowardly, in faith or in spiritual blindness and selfishness. The consequences of our actions will not affect our eternal destiny.

The Bible defines two different and distinct judgments. No one is excluded from this. What would we expect from the judgment seat of Christ? Here are three things that are going to happen. The consequence of this is everlasting separation from Heaven. The judgment of the Great White Throne is the judgment of unbelievers whose names are not written in the Book of Life. This is the Great White Judgment, where the unbelievers are judged by their deeds.

Only those who have accepted Christ as their Savior will be included in this decision. God's purpose is to reward us for the way we have lived. We will be judged for what we have achieved with our talents, skills, abilities, relationships and vocations. While sometimes we can approach life lightly, nothing in our lives is casual to God. Our entry into Heaven cost Him the death of His only begotten Son, and He has given us the Holy Spirit to inspire us to do whatever He has asked of us.

Jesus will take into account how much spiritual light we have had when we are first saved. He will also factor in the opportunities God has given us. Christ will evaluate both our motives and our works. There will be no comparisons between people because each person is uniquely created and gifted by God. We need not fear condemnation because Christ saved us from the penalty of sin. Knowing what's at stake eternally should motivate us to live a life that's obedient and pleasing to God because we will be rewarded according to the way we have lived. We are either going to be rewarded or lose reward in this judgment.

Why Is Accountability Important To Disciples?

Accountability helps to promote biblical controls or checks and balances. It provides the necessary discipline and support needed to see people reach Godly goals. While we are all ultimately accountable to God, God has established other levels of accountability to aid us in the matter of control, support, and growth. God has given the Word and the Holy Spirit as His agents of control to help provide direction and controls in our lives. When death is conquered at the close of the Millennium, then all things will come under the administration of the triune Godhead. The Son will be accountable to the One who subjected all things to him, so that God may be all in all.

> 1 Cor. 15:28 When he has done this, then the Son himself will be made subject to him who put everything under him, so that God may be all.

This in no way implies that the Son is inferior to the Father, but rather that he will be under the control of the Godhead when death is overcome. The Father, Son, and Holy Spirit are co-eternal and co-equal. Holy Spirit accepts His role as the Teacher and Comforter to come and dwell with believers.

Accountability is part of the means God uses, as will be demonstrated below. Making disciples means teaching others to obey the Lord, and this is not the easiest tack without some measure of accountability. Many fight accountability as it begins to affect their comfort zones or their self-willed agendas. Your self-will soul is at war with your spirit when you say "I think, I feel, I want". The mind, will and emotion - YOUR SOUL wants to have its way. Paul said in Galatians 2:30, *I have been crucified with Christ, and I no longer live, but Christ lives in me. (Spiritually) The life I now live in the body, I live by* **FAITH** *in the Son of God, who loved me and gave himself for me.*

The goal of accountability is not lording over people like a taskmaster. Rather, the goal is to help people grow in Christ and learn to trust in Christ. The biblical model for church leadership is a collective leadership of five-Fold ministry gifts which provides a structure for genuine accountability.

"Accountability" is applied to the whole body of Christ as a Spirit-produced and mutual responsibility to promote obedience to Christ. The Lord focused on only a few, the twelve and then the three, so the leaders should follow his example, says St. Paul. The need for accountability goes beyond the leadership and falls into a realm of "one-to-one" submission.

Paul asked why are you criticizing your brother or your sister? For we will all stand before the seat of God's judgment. Every human being, both Believers and non-believers, is accountable to a supreme God. Jesus clearly taught that a day of judgment would come when each person would be required to give an account. People are liable for both their acts and words on the Day of Judgment which will acquit or condemn them. Many reject this Scripture declaration by all manner of human rationalizations and prejudices, but their rejection cannot change the accountability truth.

Accountability is one of God's ways of bringing about solid growth and development with the right to be what God has made us for. In no way does the Bible deny our individualism but in a way that keeps each of us accountable to others. True freedom is not the right to do what one wants, which is permitted, but the power by the grace of God to do what one ought to do.

CHAPTER 2

Good Stewards of your Time

Time Management

We are to be good stewards of time and plan wisely for the future. Christian Time Management is a flourishing industry, but it is much more important for Christians to manage time. What makes Christian time management different is what we consider to be the essence of time well spent, a good place to start with is to consider how God looks at the time and what He wants us to learn from the handling of time. "I'm a clock slave — I can't even take a break!" THE DEVIL IS A LIAR !!

Moses prays, "Teach us to number our days, that we may gain a heart of wisdom". C. S. Lewis understood this: "If you read history you will find that the Christians who did the most for the present world were just those who thought most of the text "living wisely involves using our time carefully". To avoid losing focus, we need to prioritize and set goals. To delegate, recall how

Moses' father-in-law Jethro wisely taught him to delegate some of his heavy workloads?

To live as God would have us live, it is essential we make the best possible use of our allotted time. We are to spend time loving others in deed and in truth (1 John 3:17–18, 1 John 4:17-18). We need to make the most of every opportunity, making the most out of every chance to witness to others. The Bible says, *"Be very careful, then, how you live. Not as unwise but as wise" (Ephesians 5:15–16).*

God is not controlled by the time the way we humans are, but God still puts great emphasis on it. To become more like God, we need to learn to have His priorities. These are designed to teach us important lessons and to reveal His plan to us. God's priorities and plans always produce results, and so can ours. The Bible says, *"With the Lord, one day is as a thousand years, and the thousand years as one day as one thousand years"* The Sabbath is the Sabbath, but also the holy days of rest. Rest in the Lord's company.

God reveals to us what is truly most important in life. Jesus said, *"But seek first the kingdom of God and His righteousness, and all these things shall be added to you" (Matthew 6:33).* If we put money and things as equal to or higher priority than God's Kingdom, in the long run, we will have neither. We must schedule what matters most first, or it will be pushed out by the hundreds of urgent and persistent things that come at us each week.

To master being a good steward of our time is to set priorities among your goals. We need long-range plans, annual plans and daily plans, and probably several plans in between. It's not about filling every moment with busy work, but rather, organizing our time around what is important. The Bible reveals a God who is a Planner. And He wants us to be planners too. The Kingdom of God is the perfect government of God that will bring peace and plenty to this earth when Jesus Christ returns. We should be preparing for that time now. The more we prepare, the more we will receive.

God did all His work in six days and rested on the seventh, Proverbs 6:10–11 says. The Parable of the Talents shows how important it is to function diligently before the Lord arrives. Rest is not a waste of time; it is refreshment that allows us to make better use of time. Most importantly, we need to arrange a regular time with God. It is He who equips us to perform the tasks He has assigned us, and He guides our days. The worst thing we can do is treat our time as if it belonged to us, writes Paul. Time belongs to Him, so ask for His wisdom. The Bible says that, in all our efforts, our primary emphasis is on God; we cannot overlook spending time in God's presence.

The word of God indicates that we ought to reflect on what is eternal, as opposed to the fleeting pleasures of this passing life. Reflecting on your goals and using time is a healthy idea to indulge in on a daily basis. Time spent with God and getting to know Him, reading His Word and praying is never wasted. Time spent spreading the Gospel bears eternal fruit. We're expected to live as if every minute counts because it really does. It is wise to further study the topic in the Scriptures. Some consider that it is important to have their time management checked deliberately regularly. It is a good idea to list goals and responsibilities and ask God, is this His will for your life?

Proverbs 19:21 says; *Many are the plans in a man's heart, but it is the LORD's purpose that prevails. What a man desires is unfailing love; better to be poor than a liar. The fear of the LORD leads to life: Then one rests content, untouched by trouble.*

Perform with urgency and diligence. God wants us to recognize that every minute counts and should be used in a godly way In order to select the truly important. We need to act carefully, not just respond to what is desperately needed. The apostle Paul encouraged us to *"walk circumspectly, not as fools but as wise, redeeming the time, because the days are evil"* (Ephesians 5:15-16)

There's time for everything, but that doesn't mean we're going to have to do it NOW. Being a good steward of your time is a skill that helps us to control the way we and others use our own time. As a servant leader, we need to model a balanced use of time for our own good and for those we minister to. Time cannot be controlled since we are not in charge of its movement.

Good steward of Time Tips For Handling Your Time Better

1. Check out how you're spending your time: Have a week to keep a diary of your use of time (including coffee breaks, phone calls, travel time, etc.) and with whom. Then research the diary, look at recurring patterns and highlight the fact that you haven't taken your time the way you want and/or should. For example, if you spend the day in the morning, afternoon, and evening, do you work every three days? If you just had 2 of those meetings a day, will it be beneficial for the most part of the week?

2. Check out your diary with an accountability partner. Discuss the different fields and then plan to take action to resolve a few of the problems it highlights.
3. The Church of Jesus Christ encourages that the leaders of the Church should prioritize their hours. Much of their time should be spent on tasks that are relevant but not urgent. Steven Covey, a time management expert, suggests a four-box time management model that lets us make the most of our time. The four cases are "urgent," "not urgent," "important" and "not important," and the "not urgent" leaders of the Church have to devote time for them to succeed; attending meetings regularly. Should meetings always follow the same procession? Do you have to be present for meeting all the time, or only the part that needs your feedback, or when you need to hear crucial information? Will other tools help to minimize the time and duration of the daily meetings? Can you have an online review of some of the agenda items before the senior leadership meeting?
4. Set standards for response time and consideration of urgent and non-urgent issues. Speak to your team about the mutual use of time and the problems that each of you faces. Sifting through emails to read or not all of them takes time because we have many of them. Take a team approach and be able to share your time with your team.
5. Research indicates that it takes about 8 minutes to recover from being interrupted while you're in the middle of a discussion. Switch off your cell phones at meals, use your voicemail, or use a cell phone to redirect your calls. Find a time and a place where you're not going to be disturbed. Be

mindful with time, but be polite to people when managing interruptions and strive to keep interruptions to a minimum.

6. Stop procrastination by doing the worst jobs. Allocate to others some of your responsibility. It's easy to fall into the trap of thinking, "If I don't do it, it won't happen, or it won't be done as well." It might take longer to do this at the start as you have to describe what's needed, but it's worth saving time in the long run. Do the task you're putting off, split it in bits of bite-size. (How do you eat an elephant? one bite at a time).

7. Lastly, as a good steward of time, set boundaries. Having boundaries is not a bad thing; in fact, it is a good thing. A boundary simply put, is protection. Leaders are pulled into so many directions, to the point that it can affect their physical, spiritual, and mental health. It is important that a leader takes the time to spend with God to be refreshed. Jesus himself took time to be alone with God.

> **Ephesians 5:15-17** So, then, be careful how you live. Do not be unwise but wise, making the best use of your time because the times are evil. Therefore, do not be foolish, but understand what the Lord's will is.

Paul states that we as Christians are children of light now, but we live in a morally and spiritually dark world. Looking carefully requires taking the exactness and accuracy into consideration. Many Christians just sail through the minefield, unaware of the significant danger they face. They play with extreme danger, and still, they don't pay attention. Paul offers us three important things to prevent spiritual catastrophe if we want to walk carefully on this evil day.

To walk carefully in this evil day, you must use your time wisely, understand the will of the Lord, and be filled with the Holy Spirit.

Paul writes, "Therefore, look carefully how you walk, not as unwise men but as wise, redeeming the time because the days are evil". To walk spiritually pictures steady progress toward a definite goal. Without deliberate carefulness, the evil that surrounds us will overwhelm us, Paul writes. Paul urges people to write a one-sentence purpose statement for their life, based on biblically determined criteria. If you just drift through life without thinking carefully about how to spend your time, you will not end up where God wants you to be. The Bible says, "... walk in the futility of your mind, being darkened in your understanding, giving themselves over to sensuality and greed". But Christians are not to walk in that manner; we must walk carefully, he writes. The word "walk" is Paul's final use of the word "walk" in Ephesians.

1. **Paul draws the first of several contracts,** "not as unwise men, but as wise". Wisdom is a huge theme in the Bible, leaders need wisdom. James 1:5 says; *Now if any of you lacks wisdom, he should ask God, who gives generously to all without finding fault, and it will be given to him.* Lacks means falling short, being destitute or being in need. It pictures one not possessing something which is necessary.

James does not want his readers to be deficient in anything that reflects Christian maturity. Wisdom is the ability to judge correctly and to follow the best course of action, based on knowledge and understanding. The Bible tells us the godly character qualities that we need to develop. God gave Moses the plan for the tabernacle, and skillful men crafted the beautiful final product. We must follow God's directions if we want our lives to be beautiful for Him. The only way to accomplish this is to follow the example of divine wisdom, given to us in Scripture.

"Making the most of your time" (5:16a) is literally, "redeeming the time." To redeem means to buyback. The idea is that God gives us choice moments to seize for His purposes. To walk carefully in this dark world, you must use your time wisely. You must say no to hours of TV or computer games in order to say yes to reading and studying God's Word. You must be alert to His purposes and ready to grab those opportunities like a shrewd business person sees an opportunity for a profit and grabs it. For the unbeliever, life is in bondage to futility and meaninglessness. But the Christian can buy back those otherwise wasted hours and use the opportunities for eternal significance. He can be a steward of his resources for God's kingdom purposes, investing wisely in opportunities to further the gospel around the globe. He is a Steward of the times he spends to bring others to know Christ and grow in Him. He rears his children to know and follow Christ.

2. **Paul says Lord's will is the navigation** in Ephesians 5:17, *"Do not be reckless, but realize what the Lord's will is"* In life, the Lord's will is the navigation map that tells us where we are heading and how to get there. It would be reckless to set out to sea with no idea of where to go or how to get there. The Lord wants you to understand His will in order to keep your life going.

To understand this means to grasp with the mind. This implies some effort on your part. The Lord's will is revealed in His Word, and Paul has mentioned it several times in Ephesians. God's will relates to His eternal purpose to be glorified by summing up all things in Christ. He does this by saving His elect (Jews and Gentiles) and bringing both groups together as one. You must receive a revelation on purpose with your mind so that you can live your life in line with it. The Church manifests His wisdom to the rulers and authorities in the heavenly places. The Bible says, "We have been predestined according to His purpose who works all things after the counsel of His will." The will of God or your will. Remember, "I think", "I want" and "I Feel" is your will.

3. **Paul admonished: You must live daily in light of God's purpose to be glorified in Christ through His Church**. If God is working out His eternal purpose through the Church, then His people must be committed to the Church. Paul says that to be casual in your connection to the Church is not to be devoted to what God is committed to. The will of the Lord includes bringing the gospel to the lost so that they may be saved and incorporated into

the Church, he says. In that way, His glory is manifested all over the earth, as former rebels are reconciled to God and to one another through the cross, Paul writes. If you're just living to get a good job, pay the bills, and enjoy selfish pursuits, with an occasional trip to Church when it doesn't interfere with your entertainment program, Paul calls you foolish. To walk carefully in this dark world, you must not be foolish, but understand what the will of the Lord is and apply it to how you live each day.

In order to walk carefully, you must be filled with the Holy Spirit.

Paul gives another comparison, "And do not be drunk with wine, for that is dissipation, but be filled with the Spirit." Grammatically, this is followed by five participants who demonstrate the effects of being filled with the Spirit: speaking, singing, making music, giving thanks, and being subject to one another. The first and the last concern our actions towards one another. The second, third, and fourth concern our conduct towards the Lord. The past participle also defines and rules the relationship section between husbands and wives, parents and children, and slaves and masters (5:22-6:9).

Being filled with the Spirit is an ongoing experience that empowers us for godliness and service. To be filled with wine, you give yourself over to the wine and keep drinking, Paul writes. The believers should be under the control or influence of the Holy Spirit, not the other way around. We should take the positive command to be filled with the Spirit just as seriously as we take the negative command not to be drunk, he writes. It should be the normative daily experience of every Believer, he says. It is essentially the same thing as walking by means of the Spirit (Gal. 5:16) and gives us victory over the flesh and produces the fruit of the Spirit in us. The Bible says, "Be continually filled" and "Be filled" in the verb tense, which means "controlling the Spirit" (5:18). The word "control" means "to be filled" or "controlled" by the Spirit, which is the same as saying, "I am filled with God." The Person of the Holy Spirit Lives inside of me. You can find out more about the Holy Spirit in my teaching *"The Person with Power: Holy Spirit Dwelling on the Inside Book by Teresa S. McCurry*

Paul lists singing, thankfulness, and mutual submission as results of being filled by the Spirit. "Being subject to one another in fear of Christ" does not do away with proper spheres of authority. Christ had a right to remain in glory in heaven, but he willingly laid aside that right to serve as a servant. We should have that same attitude, submitting ourselves to one another as we outdo one another in love. The three different terms for songs indicate variety, and singing infers at least a measure of exuberance and joy. The word "love" is the opposite of grumbling and complaining, and it is to be thankful for all of God's goodness in all things, even when we may not be able to understand His immediate purpose.

> **Proverbs 27:1 Do not boast about tomorrow, for you do not know what a day may bring.**

A good life is a collection of godly days put together. Make sure that today is the best day in the chain. Are you living today as godly as you do, and are you pleased with what God has given you?

Business and other plans should be submitted to God's sovereign will, for only He knows tomorrow. Children and youths foolishly and impatiently presume on many tomorrows, for they crave imagined future pleasures rather than appreciate today. There always more excuses. Most men boast of tomorrow in various ways. It will take care of itself. You should count each day a gift and use it wisely to the glory of God's glory.

Don't boast about tomorrow: its human nature to be overly confident about what's going on in the future. We don't know what's going to happen tomorrow, so we should have a humble attitude towards the future. And always remember **GOD IS IN CONTROL!!**

— CHAPTER 3 —

SPEAK LIFE: COMMUNICATING EFFECTIVELY

According to Wikipedia: *Communication* is the act of conveying meanings from one entity or group to another through the use of mutually understood signs, symbols, and semiotic rules.

Communication is, in fact, a very complicated matter. It can be influenced by a wide range of factors, including our emotions and place. Strong communication skills are considered to be essential for ministry leaders. In reality, precise, efficient and unmistakable communication is not the easy thing to do.

The various communications types include: spoken or verbal Communication, Written Communication, non-verbal communication and visualization. Body language, expressions, how we dress or behave, where we stand and even our fragrance can convey messages. Voice tone and voice tone may offer clues to the mood or emotional state. Hand signals or gestures may lead to a spoken message.

There is more to effective communication than merely sharing information. It is about knowing the meaning behind the feelings and actions. You will need to listen in a way that acquires the full sense of what's being said. These skills will deepen the relationships and develop greater faith and respect for others.1 Thessalonians 5:12 says; And we urge you, brethren, to recognize those who labor among you, and are over you in the Lord and [a]admonish you, They can also promote teamwork, problem-solving, and your overall mental and social wellbeing. Communicating more clearly and efficiently requires, for many of us, acquiring some essential skills.

Communication in the church can be described as the use of words, acts, emotions, presence, moods, signs, communion and prayers to expose the work of God's redemption in our lives and create closer relationships with God.

The purpose of all divine communication is to unite people with God. Every elder, deacon, teacher, pastor, evangelist, prophet and Apostle Church volunteer is an instrument of communication in the church. We all need to learn to communicate, understand, and learn to grow with one another. We, as instruments of communication, must be careful not to use the mediums of communication to draw attention to ourselves, our beauty, our achievements or our gifts and abilities as we speak life to encourage our sisters and brothers.

We have to consider the impact our words can have on other people. God created us to be passionate beings, and the Bible tells us that our words hold the power of life and death

(Proverbs 18:21 The tongue has the power of life and death, and those who love it will eat its fruit.). Encouragement often comes through spoken words. So does discouragement. *"The words of the reckless pierce like swords, but the tongue of the wise brings healing."* (Proverbs 12:18), but *"how good is a timely word!"* (Proverbs 15:23). To speak life, we encourage, edify, and speak blessing to others by what we say.

Proverbs 10:11 says that *"the mouth of the righteous is a fountain of life."* How can we, as believers learn to monitor our words so that we speak life to those we love and to this lost world in such desperate need of hope?

Those who purpose to speak life understand that the words we speak have consequences. When a witness testifies in court, their words may decide whether a defendant lives or dies. Our words can affect the emotional and spiritual health of someone we care about. we have to ask ourselves whether we are inspiring people with hope or crushing them with judgement and condemnation.

The word of God tells us that our words originate from inside our hearts: *"For out of the abundance of the heart the mouth speaks. The good person out of his good treasure brings forth good, and the evil person out of his evil treasure brings forth evil. I tell you, on the day of judgment people will give account for every careless word they speak, for by your words you will be justified, and by your words, you will be condemned"* (Matthew 12:34–37). Careless words are tossed out unthinkingly, but heaven hears them. If we don't mean it, we should not say it..

In seeking spiritual maturity, we must keep the communication line between God and ourselves open and the communication lines among ourselves open. Understanding that, think of your relationship with God. The way you talk, pray, seek to know Him, look to Him for guidance and steps of obedience; this is your "vertical" relationship with Him. The same can be said of your horizontal relationships (the people around you) when your vertical relationship (with God) is not in place or is wavering. *All* of your earthly relationships, whether you know it or acknowledge it, are held up or let down by the condition of your vertical relationship with God. If your relationship with God is not in the right place, all of the relationships with the people in your life will be affected or fall. **All of them.**

The only tool church leaders can use to guide Christ's church is their ability to communicate and to communicate effectively, the word of God, and the word of the church must be kept open.

A church that lacks effective communication becomes a house that is divided against itself. What kind of communication steps do we need for the church to glow with love and righteousness? We need communication steps to build, maintain and enjoy strong fellowship with God and each other Remember what Jesus said just before He gave up His life on the cross? "It is finished." Scholars and theologians have examined and unpacked what He said at that moment for centuries, trying to understand what Jesus truly meant.

> **Ephesians 4:29, (NIV)** "Do not let any unwholesome talk come out of your mouths, but only what helps build others up according to their needs, that it may benefit those who listen.

As leaders, it is important to communicate with God first and then with people. That is the order which will achieve the highest level of production. The cross is both vertical and horizontal because we need both to live how God intended. Vertically, we have to have a connection and relationship with Christ. Horizontally, we are made to be in community with others and have relationships with one another. Without a relationship with God, our earthly relationships will fail. Without our earthly friendships, we are missing out on a huge part of life that God intends for us to take part in.

Sometimes our life is going great, and we are doing well in all our relationships, while sometimes we do both of them halfheartedly. But what we need to strive for, is to be at the center of the cross where we are committed to loving both.

When leaders do not communicate with God first: they appear to rely too heavily on their knowledge, which often leads to problems. Trusting in God brings prosperity and sound guidance. We are the body of Christ, and we all are a piece of the plan. It is a collaborative effort. We have to love vertically so that in turn, we can love horizontally and show Christ's love to those around us. Now, our love will not be near as strong as His because His love is unchanging and never failing. But we are called to love like Jesus, and that is loving without boundaries. We are not called to be perfect, but to be set apart.

That universal symbol conveys a message of what is to come and what life truly should display: a cross.

> Jesus said, "Take up your cross every day, and follow me" (Luke 9:23).

Can't over-stress on the importance of interacting with God and people. When leaders learn to speak life in any given situation, we tend to see positive results in that situation. We have to love vertically so that in turn, we can love horizontally and show Christ's love to those around us. Now, our love will not be near as strong as His because His love is unchanging and never failing. Bit we are called to love like Jesus, and that is loving without boundaries. We are not called to be perfect, but to be set apart.

That universal symbol conveys a message of what is to come and what life truly should display: a cross.

Communication skills

The principle is the key to effective interpersonal communication. "Seek first to understand, then to be understood" is key to understanding, In Proverbs 18:13, we read, *"He who answers before listening is his folly and his shame."*

- **Learning how to listen**

Some leaders spend time and energy cultivating new skills, such as long-term planning, time management and public speaking. But what about taking the time to improve listening skills? The ability will be built by those who wish to be good leaders.

Practice the art of active listening. Active listening is an expression of your value for the person. It means that you unselfishly put your interests on hold for a time and concentrate on the speaker's deeds and words.

- **Have a specific objective here.**

Good communication begins with a specific reason for contact. You need to know what you want to say before you can communicate effectively. Communication is more than just talking about it. If you just don't understand what you're trying to say, you're not going to be able to express it to anyone. The more significant the conversation, the more carefully you think about and prepare what you're going to say.

> Matthew 12:37. For by your words, you will be acquitted, and by your words, you will be condemned."

Before they Speak, wise leaders think so they can subdue frustration rather than stoke it up. In the New Testament James says, "Everyone should be swift to hear, slow to speak, and slow to get angry," these three commands may be the most often disobeyed commands in the bible. However, if viewed frequently, they can dramatically alter a human's life; It will help bring about the just life God wants.

- **Speak honestly**

You can pass on confidence to your listener when you provide a model of open communication. Let the emotions you have about the message you are sharing express them. Note, the goal is not to "get it off your chest" but to say what is in the other person's best interest.

- **Create A Ministry feedback system:**

The best feedback is precise, descriptive and focuses on habits which can be altered. Develop a communications strategy to provide accurate, Weekly updates to those who need to be updated. Once covid 19 hit we had weekly senior leader meetings because things were changing every day. We had to seek God then put his plan into action ….just giving feedback will help prevent the humiliation and lack of support that often happens when team members are left uninformed about some ministry changes.

- Communicate more than you believe you can. Be repeatable, routine, habitual, and enduring. To err on the side of too much contact is better than too little. Be vigilant. Be sensitive.

- Not all communication has to be profound. Relationships progress through various levels with an appropriate depth of contact at each level. Church leaders are often required to communicate at a personal center far beyond the level of relationship they have developed with the listener.

Why Are These Skills Essential?

Everyone Communicates, Few Connect. John Maxwell teaches that communication must include both information and inspiration that the content and ability to communicate well is key to a leader's ability to connect with their audience.

> Psalm 19:14 NIV [14] May these words of my mouth and this meditation of my heart be pleasing in your sight, Lord, my Rock and my Redeemer.

David wishes that his words were appropriate to the Lord. David was the man after God's own heart for he knew that it is not only the outside of a cup that needs to be clean and unsullied, but God desires an inside purity, which comes from a heart that is submitted before the Lord and rivers of living water will flow. A heart that meditates on the Lord and lifts up Jesus, is the one that shows an inner grace and beauty, you have to be willing to be transformed into the likeness of the Christ, for out of the mouth come thoughts that are conceived in the heart.

Benefits Of Being An Effective Communicator

Communication is vital to any relationship, whether at home, work, ministry or any other place where we interact with other people. Jesus used various tools to communicate principles and ideologies that pointed to the Kingdom of God and Himself. In the same way, we can improve practically every area of our lives through good communication.

Value Transparency:

If we can better articulate our beliefs, it's easier to bring people with us into one page and head in the direction we want them to head. Effective communication is essential to achieving results, whether in marriage, parenting, leadership, evangelism, or business.

Following the ministry of Paul and Barnabas,

> Acts 14:1 tells us, "Now they entered the Jewish synagogue together at Iconium, and talked in such a way that a great number of both Jews and Greeks believed."

Yeah, there is space for God to travel, but God moves by helping us develop communication skills several times over.

Communication skills do not only include the way we say things but also what we say. If our words are misleading, what we said will eventually kill people and organizations. Can our interpersonal skills contribute to greater authenticity? If we can express facts well, with the same points, we will be able to help people motivate themselves.

Paul says in 1 Thessalonians 4:16,

> "That is why one another encourages with these words."

Words are little other than words. They hold the power of life and death. The way we use them will decide whether or not we will provide meaningful motivation, exhortation and edification. Encouragement comes most frequently through verbal communication and actions. If we are successfully delivering a message of hope to others, it can go a long way. If we motivate a peer, colleague or mentee, the strength of our encouragement is directly influenced by our communication skills.

Communication Errors In The Church

Church communications failures can have more effect than what is transmitted. Leadership does not interact efficiently; conflicts occur; tension introduces itself and delays the Ministries momentum. As Leaders (as well as volunteers) understand what is happening within the church, and why, they feel respected and engaged. Staff feel ignored and undervalued when decisions are taken that are not shared.

Zero Communication may have a massive effect on the work of other persons. Before it is launched, Church leadership needs to think about who will be affected by a new initiative. Team members tend to do a good job and can take the opportunity to learn about projects that will affect their jobs and responsibilities.

They are controlling who is getting information. Church leaders often monitor who has access to what knowledge, because it somehow makes them feel more secure to know something other people don't.

This hoarding of information will cause problems on the team, mostly when workers are not provided with the critical information necessary to do their job.

Churches commit communication mistakes. There's a delicate balance between revealing enough information to help the team members move forward with something and revealing sensitive details that may not be appropriate or important.

When a church is experiencing challenging times, and significant changes are going on, it is even more important to communicate the specifics with team members. It is vital to establish a predictable process for sharing information. For example, members of the team might expect to hear from the senior pastor or business administrator about significant church changes, yet their immediate supervisor may share information about significant changes. All parties involved should know what information is shared and who the communicator of data will be.

Healthy churches communicate well. They recognize that it is almost impossible to speak too much. Communication is more than making announcements or designing a Facebook page. It is a core process with many related components.

A fair communication process begins before there is anything to announce. Church initiatives and changes almost always derive from a decision. The more people you include in developing a decision, the more people you have that can inform others about that decision. By doing so, you enlist a wider group of informed advocates who can speak about a decision and answer questions asked by people you might never encounter.

The more channels you use to disseminate information, the harder it is to keep facts accurate. One person may be responsible for posting an event to Facebook, while another develops a newsletter. The process of checking and rechecking times and locations are as mundane as it is crucial. Changing the time of a meeting or event may not seem like a significant issue to you, but it may be to individuals.

Alignment of what we do with what we say. Policies that are unequally applied procedures that are ignored and information provided to a few carry damaging unspoken messages. This can undermine relationships and trust. The letter should be consistent, consistent and consistent.

Communication is essential, especially in every aspect of the ministry. Lack of Communication can lead to a host of issues on any auxiliary.

- **Misunderstandings:** Out of a lack of communication can lead to severe issues in the church. A worker might misunderstand what their responsibilities are if they're not spelt out. They might then not do their job as well as they could be if they fully understood. If a new church worker/ team member isn't properly boarded, they might misunderstand their place in the body of Christ. Failure to communicate can lead to missed opportunities, especially at work. It may be because an employee does not clearly express their interest in a promotion opportunity, a manager may have an opening or an opportunity for an employee they are not communicating well.

- **Unnecessary conflicts** can arise as a result of lack of communication. In the church, you have people trying too hard to do things individually because they don't communicate well with their team. Members overwork themselves where it's not necessary, and by the end of it all they find out that they all did the same thing without communicating with one another, this can lead to conflict as they start bickering about who caused the other to waste their time and about who was too lazy the other person had to take up their tasks. Same applies to the cooperate world for example,

- **Transmission of information:** Have you ever heard of the grapevine effect? The grapevine is the informal transmission of information, gossip or rumor from person to person. The term originated during early Civil War days when the telegraph wires resembled grapevines. The grapevine provides an outlet for imagination and truth-seeking. A lack of communication can lead to the "grapevine" effect, also known as the "telephone game." If one person miscommunicates information, that information can quickly be passed.

- **Lack of Communication** in a whole variety of contexts can lead to distrust in the Church. Members of the Church could not believe the Church will treat them safely. Bad contact often limits the closeness of their relationships within the church body. It also affects the ways the members interact with each other.

- When a church member errs and is being corrected, and the message is in such a way that is not encouraging or loving that member starts to feel discouraged about things and starts to lose their self-esteem. Even the bible admonished us to correct with love, hating the sin and not the sinner.

Some church leaders do not know how to go about correcting faulty members or workers, they do this in such a blunt way that the person ends up too ashamed even to show their face in church, and if they do come, they lose the spirit to participate because they suddenly feel judged. (I was so guilty of being blunt and brutally honest. If you don't know me you might think I still am. I really had to seek God about being a more gentle leader, I prayed for the fruit of the spirit to become more prevalent in my life). James 1:19: *So then, my beloved brethren, let every man be swift to hear, slow to speak, slow to wrath.* I had to seek the Holy Spirit for guidance before I confronted someone.

―――― CHAPTER 4 ――――

QUALIFIED LEADERS TO ASSIST YOU: DELEGATION OF TASKS

Delegating refers to sharing or transition of roles within leadership positions. Delegating at every level is a vital skill for the overseer. Learning due to fears of giving up power or lack of trust, maybe a big challenge for some leaders.

By delegating work to others, the individual transfers work to people whose skills suit the task(s) better, thereby enhancing the productivity of the team members who entrust the work and decreasing their stress. Delegating can be an integral aspect of coaching and training others. It is one significant way to help them learn new skills. Delegating tasks to others allows you the time and opportunity to concentrate on higher-level activities. Develops confidence among staff and facilitates communication.

> Matthew 8:9 (NIV): For I am a man under authority, with soldiers under me. I tell this one, 'Go,' and he goes; and that one, 'Come,' and he comes. I say to my servant, 'Do this,' and he does it.

In verse above, Jesus was eager and ready to enter the house of the Roman centurion, to cure the servant of the man. However, the centurion objected to this, claiming that he was not worthy of having Jesus in his house. The soldier knew that Jesus was a man with great power and connection with God. He saw that the healings of Jesus did not resemble the attempted supernatural works of the pagans of his day. Jesus just talked, and it was over. That was the confidence they should have shown in Him, Jesus should be showing them, he says. The Jewish people should have regarded him as having the legitimacy that they wanted to believe in him. The bible states that he did so because he was the one with authority.

Delegation of tasks has been one topic that the bible has always encourage since the book of Genesis, and the Lord has enabled his anointed to pick out people who are worthy and skilful and assign them tasks to do that way lessening the burden of the job on the selected head. Many people where privileged to be chosen by great men of the anointing of old we had the Apostles, the disciples and so many others each man and woman appointed a task to run for a given period.

And like every well-functioning Ministry today, the Holy Spirit had a way of checking up on each person to make sure they all performed their tasks diligently and can complete what they started. The church today we have pastors, evangelist, prophets, teachers elders, deacons and ushers, and many other auxiliary units. Down to security and hospitality. Each person assigned a simple task to complete from time to time, and each task geared towards making the church work smoothly.

Naturally, no man can do all these things, no matter how strong and agile the head overseer is, they can not preach and counsel and clean the church and provide security to the church all by himself. He has to recruit the help of other individuals in the church and assign the tasks to help the church function smoothly. And he also monitors these people or gets reports from the department heads.

Delegating; What Does The Bible Say?

> Exodus 18:13-26 ESV The next day Moses sat to judge the people, and the people stood around Moses from morning till evening. When Moses' father-in-law saw all that he was doing for the people, he said, "What is this that you are doing for the people? Why do you sit alone, and all the people stand around you from morning till evening?" And Moses said to his father-in-law, "Because the people come to me to inquire of God; when they have a dispute, they come to me, and I decide between one person and another, and I make them know the statutes of God and his laws." Moses' father-in-law said to him, "What you are doing is not good. ..."

> 2 Timothy 2:2 ESV And what you have heard from me in the presence of many witnesses entrust to faithful men who will be able to teach others also.

> Titus 1:5 ESV This is why I left you in Crete so that you might put what remained into order, and appoint elders in every town as I directed you—

In Exodus chapter 18, we are told of how Moses himself did everything in his ministry. Jethro, the father-in-law of Moses, sent him some sage guidance and encouragement. Put simply, and he'd been told to create depth! We must give our volunteers the same opportunity people gave us to learn by doing the ministry hands-on. It can deter you from doing what only you can do while you are doing something that others can do. That's when you'll hear, "Well done, my good and faithful servant." By doing what some can't do if you do it in a hands-on way, you can get better in ministry. The bible teaches us that the secret to the success of ministry is delegation, and it also happens in the church and the Bible.

The Twelve called together all the disciples and said, "It would not be right for us to abandon the ministry of God's Word to wait on tables." The disciples turned the duties of ministry over from among them to seven men. Jethro warned Moses of this very thing in Exodus 18:21-22. Defining the vision, evaluation, or fruit inspection are projects only the leader should do. That will make your load lighter, because they will share it with you. Once a task has been delegated a leader should not just fold their hands and expect that the person they chose will do the work effectively and do it well, No in fact according to Jethro's advice the leader is encouraged to supervise them. You have to inspect what you expect. Take weekly, monthly and quarterly reports and make sure you check up on them to see that they are doing what they need to do and are doing it well.

The job of supervising the tasks cannot be assigned to simply anyone because frankly, it is the leader that has been given the vision it is up to him to trust those things that he feels others can do the job, so he can focus on what is essential things only him/her can do. And one of those crucial things is supervising to see that the vision is not lost.

Tips to Effective Delegation

- **Identify what you have to do:** Let's have a look at Acts 6:2 "Then the Twelve gathered all the disciples together and said, 'To wait on tables, it would not be right for us to ignore the ministry of the Word of God.'" The disciples were not too friendly to wait on tables, but this mission stopped them from what they had to do. There are tons of good ideas and projects that prevent us from doing the projects motivated and guided by God that He has for us. Training, directing, managing, and hiring is more critical than teaching, singing, performing, and being the only individual associated with the children.

- **Identify and let others do things they can.** Start with jobs that you do that others could do if they were educated and taught correctly. Next, if individuals were no issue, recognize places you might use a worker. Do not assume the same actions will yield different results because the same steps will still produce the same results. You must be able to do what you have never done if you want what you have never had! The same goes for any volunteer. Without allowing others to have playtime, you can't produce depth!

- There were requirements needed to do the job, like being full of the spirit and full of wisdom, Moses was told. The disciples didn't turn this responsibility over to just anybody; they found people from among them. It was not a once a month job but something that was an all-time commitment. A primary rule of delegation is qualified and whom you delegate responsibilities. Are they capable and able? Define what you want to be done. Everyone needs a job description, especially volunteers. They also need checklists to show them what you want them to do. Remember always to do what is best for the children and not what is only best for adults.

- Exodus 18:20 advises us to *"teach them the laws and decrees and show them how to live and how to perform their duties."* Hands-on instruction is better than lectures. It is essential that, along with accountability, you always delegate authority. There are plenty of places for the buck to end when you grant other people power. In the training and equipping process, everybody can support. In the end, the buck doesn't stop.

- If they don't have your heart, a person can't represent you well; Always take someone with you whenever you can. Develop outstanding communication lines. Enable someone to be better at what they are doing, any chance that you get. Repeatedly say thank you. In a well-done job, compliment your volunteers. Building a support network around your volunteers is essential. It isn't as complicated as you might think.

- And lastly, Make corrections and modifications where necessary. Every service can be improved if you make modifications and corrections every week. Give an example for your volunteers to pursue, and a model worth imitating. Always set the rhythm, be the master. Be the kind of person you want to be working with, oddly lead no matter what.

Delegation: Why Some Leaders Refuse It.

One of the biggest reasons for stalled growth, low morale of teams, and not sustaining momentum has to do with leaders who refuse to delegate. They only want, either for personal or official reasons they feel that they can do it all and do not need to have other people doing their job.

Delegation doesn't mean a leader can dump responsibilities and run. They have to be available to assist, advise and encourage. Some leaders feel if they are going to be involved in a task, they might as well do it themselves which ends up wrong for them, at the end of the day they are overworked and do not produce results hence the importance of delegation.

The delegation, if it should be done right, means they give up the right to control every outcome, and some people just can't seem to be able to trust full control of a project to their team members. Some people just don't know how to trust people with work they feel others won't do it right or the way they want it done so they tell you to manage this project but 70% of the time they are all over you trying to control the outcome.

Ever worked with someone who wants to embrace all the glory for themselves, so they perform 90% or more of the task? Some leaders are just like that; they find it hard to share the spotlight with people. They want to be the most liked, most praised, most talked about in church. They want it all for themselves and having someone else do the job for them is merely going to be in the way of their shine, so they won't delegate that tasks even if the person will do it better, they would instead do it alone.

God knows that the work needs to be done and he for sure knows that just one man cannot achieve it, so he sent out many, some to plant and some to harvest.

When it comes to delegation of tasks, one must understand how to go about it. You have to know that when delegating there are some facts that you just have to keep in mind.

First, Authority Can Be Assigned. As a leader, you can transfer pieces of your formal authority to another teammate, like in your absence you pick someone to oversee a project and that person can relay the feedback to you when assigning a task to that person. In essence, you can deputize your teammate to take action on your behalf within the boundaries of the delegated (transferred) authority.

Authority chiefly comes from the power of position. The more authority you have, the greater your ability to delegate higher-level, more meaningful and challenging tasks to others to help them learn, develop, and grow. Think of it as a pyramid of authority that can delegate tasks to anyone below its rank, thereby spreading the work and allowing each member to participate and contribute to the body's development.

Secondly, when delegating you have to keep at the back of your mind that: Responsibility may not be charged, but may be assigned.

As a leader, you can assign responsibilities to a teammate in terms of the results that need to be achieved. However, you need to keep in mind that you only posted commitment to your teammate.

Assigned responsibility should be made in terms of the goals or results to be accomplished, not the detailed specifics for doing the job. As a leader, you must know that whatever comes out of a task either excellent or bad it's on you, so with this in mind when assigning tasks to your team members you should match the job to the ability of the person. Give less complicated assignments to the newbies something you know that if they mess it up, you can provide a remedy and provide it fast. And the more difficult tasks should be given to more experienced members who are experts in what they do. Don't give out the job to people out of partiality or because you trying to get in their good graces.

And thirdly before delegating learn to hold people accountable for every job they do.

Accountability Means Obligation

Accountability is the moral compulsion felt by a teammate to meet the goals and objectives of an assigned task. As a result of accepting a task assignment, your teammate in effect gives you a promise either expressed or implied—to do her best in carrying out the activities associated with it. Having taken on the task you assigned to them, your teammate is obligated to complete it and is held accountable for the results produced. Don't let failure slide just because you like a person or because you are very close to that person, once you start doing that really, that person will not learn and will not grow and other team members will either start complaining or also follow in that footstep because they know you won't hold them accountable for their actions

With the same energy, you use in celebrating success, use the same power to call out errors and have offending members make the adjustments.

Some Authorities Delegated In The Bible:

Authority Delegated to Christ Jesus: Jesus taught with authority. *"And it came to pass when Jesus had ended these sayings, and the people were astonished at his doctrine: For he taught them as [one] having authority, and not as the scribes."* (Matt. 7:28, 29). Jesus' authority is greater than that of Moses or the prophets. (Matt. 17:1-5).

Before Jesus ascended up on high, Matthew records, *"And Jesus came and spoke unto them, saying,* **"All power (authority) is given unto me in heaven and earth"** *(Matt.28:18)*. Jesus has all authority in heaven and earth NOW!

Peter declares Moses' prophecy and Jesus' assertive fulfilment indeed finds realization in Jesus, *"For Moses truly said unto the fathers, A prophet shall the Lord your God raise unto you of your brethren, like unto me; he shall ye hear in all things whatsoever he shall say unto you. And it shall come to pass, [that] every soul, which will not hear that prophet, shall be destroyed from among the people"* (Acts 3:22, 23). Jesus is the authorized prophet of God!

The Hebrew writer proclaims this prophet is Jesus, the Son of God. *"God, who at sundry times and in divers' manners spoke in time past unto the fathers by the prophets, Hath in these last days spoken unto us by [his] Son, whom he hath appointed heir of all things, by whom also he made the worlds"* (Hebrews 1:1, 2). Thus, Jesus is God's authorized Spokesmen for this age! Moreover, the apostle Paul teaches that this power (authority) will remain with Jesus until He (Jesus) comes again. *"Then [cometh] the end, when he shall have delivered up the kingdom to God, even the Father; when he shall have put down all rule and all authority and power" (1 Corinthians 15:24).* If one will not listen to Jesus, he will be destroyed. Therefore, Jesus Christ must have all authority in our lives if we will be pleasing to the Heavenly Father.

Jesus Delegates Authority to his Apostles by the Holy Spirit: "Go ye therefore, and teach all nations, baptizing them in the name of the Father, and of the Son, and the Holy Ghost" (Matt. 28:19).

The Lord's Prayer recorded while hanging on the cross, *"For I have given unto them the words which thou gavest me..."* (John 17:8). These words were to be remembered with the help of the Holy Spirit by revelation. *"Howbeit when he, the Spirit of truth, is come, he will guide you into all truth: for he shall not speak of himself; but whatsoever he shall hear, [that] shall he speak: and he will shew you things to come"* (John 16:13; 1 Corinthians 2:11-13). Paul in Ephesians 3:5 says, *"Which in other ages was not made known to the sons of men, as it is now revealed unto his holy apostles and prophets by the Spirit."* Furthermore, Paul by the Spirit proclaims, *"If any man thinks himself to be a prophet, or spiritual, let him acknowledge that the things that I write unto you are the commandments of the Lord"* (1 Corinthians 14:37).

Thus, from these Scriptures, the apostles were to carry out the commission of Jesus who received all authority from the Heavenly Father. Jesus sent the apostles with the words that He received. The apostles were guided by the Holy Spirit what they said and what they wrote. (Matthew 10:19; 2 Timothy 3:16, 17). If one will not accept the writings of the apostles, who were sent by Jesus, fails to receive Christ (John 17:8; 2 Corinthians 13:5).

Apostles Delegate Authority: Paul wrote to Timothy, "And the things that thou hast heard of me among many witnesses, the same commit thou to faithful men, who shall be able to teach others also" (2 Timothy 2:2). Apostolic writings are a part of the Scriptures (2 Peter 3:15, 16). Their reports give us insight into the things of God (Ephesians 3:4; 1 Corinthians 2:10-13). Today when one preaches the pure and unadulterated Word of God, he is preaching that which is to free man from sin (John 8:31, 32; 17:17). All will be judged by this word! (John 12:48). One must preach this word without addition or subtraction or be accursed (Galatians 1:6-10; Revelation 20:11-15).

Authority - Primary and Delegated: Only God has absolute authority - primary - All other power is that which He has delegated. He delegated authority to His Son, to apostles and prophets who wrote the bible. Delegated authority is binding. If we can understand that, it will never replace the higher authority of God and His Word. We must recognize this and accept authority where God has placed it.

CHAPTER 5

Disagreement with your Brother/Sister

Conflict Resolution

The word of God has many commands to the believers that are indicative of living at peace with one another. We are instructed to love one another: *John 13:34; "This commandment I give to you, that you love one another; as I have loved you, that you also love one another".*

We are also encouraged to live in peace and harmony with one another (Hebrews 12:14) *"Pursue peace with all people, and holiness, without which no one will see the Lord",* to settle our differences among ourselves *(2 Corinthians 13:11),* to be patient, kind, and tenderhearted toward one another (1 Corinthians 13:4), to consider others before ourselves (Philippians 2:3), to bear one another's burdens (Ephesians 4:2), and to rejoice in the truth (1 Corinthians 13:6). Conflict is the other side of the coin of Christian behavior as outlined in Scripture.

There are times when, despite all efforts to reconcile, various issues prevent us from resolving conflict in the church. There are two places in the New Testament that clearly and unmistakably address conflict resolution where sin is involved. In Matthew 18:15-17, Jesus gives the steps for dealing with a sinning brother. According to this passage, in the event of conflict involving overt sin, we are to address it one-on-one first, then if still unresolved it should be taken to a small group, and finally before the whole church if the problem still remains.

According to Wikipedia; conflict is a clash of interest. The basis of friction may vary, but it is always a part of society. Cause of conflict may be personal, racial, class, caste, political and international. Conflict in groups often follows a specific course. In the cooperate world, there are three kinds of conflict.

- Task conflict
- Relationship conflicts and
- Value conflicts
- Self conflicts

The first of the three types of conflict in the workplace, task conflict often involves concrete issues related to employees' work assignments. It can include disputes about how to divide up resources, differences of opinion on procedures and policies. Leaders can serve as de facto mediators by identifying the deeper interests underlying parties' positions. Try to engage the parties in a collaborative problem-solving process in which they brainstorm possible solutions. When parties develop solutions together, they are more likely to abide by the agreement and get along better in the future.

In organizations, people who would not ordinarily meet in real life are often thrown together. It's no surprise that relationship conflict can be expected in organizations. Invite a colleague out to lunch and try to get to know him or her better. Discovering things you have in common may help bring you together. If the conflict persists or worsens, enlist the help of a manager in resolving your differences.

Disputes involving values tend to heighten defensiveness, distrust, and alienation. Parties can feel so strongly about standing by their values that they reject trades that would satisfy other interests. Aim for a cognitive understanding in which you and your coworker reach an accurate conceptualization of one another's point of view. You may be able to reframe a values-based dispute by appealing to other values that you, your counterpart share, writes Lawrence Susskind in an article in a Negotiation Briefings newsletter.

Conflict resolution is conceptualized as the methods and processes involved in facilitating the peaceful ending of conflict and retribution. Conflict is a standard part of every human existence on earth. It usually results when our desires, expectations, fears or wants collide with the desires, expectations, fears or wants of others. Ina simple sentence, conflict is the difference in opinion or purpose that frustrates an individual's or group's goals and desires.

Conflicts can arise in all sectors of life, and the church is no exception. Wherever you have different people with different opinions, there is bound to be a conflict of interests. So, what causes these conflicts in the church?

Conflict in the church is nothing new. It has been in existence since the beginning of the New Testament church in the first century. In the book of Acts 6, some Apostles had dealt with a dispute that had arisen from the early church. This conflict dealt with favoritism between two classes of people. There are five reasons found in Acts 6:1-2 that shows how conflict can be fueled within a congregation.

1. When new people are added to a congregation it can cause conflict as people find it hard to adjust to the presence of new people, so during this period, they tend to have a significant conflict of interests with the old trying to maintain what they have always known and the new trying to introduce new methods but not being able to get through to the senior members.

2. Another reason for conflict, according to Acts 6, is change. Yes, good old change almost everyone has a problem adjusting to a change in their routine, change can be a very bitter adversary. But change can be useful, and it can also be harmful. Conflict in the church can arise when there is a change from what used to be precisely the old rules have existed for years, and you trying to introduce something new will automatically face some kind of rejection.

3. There were two distinct communities in Acts 6: the Hebraic Jews and the Hellenistic Jews. These two communities shared a similar religion, because of their backgrounds, they differed in several respects. This conduct also happens within congregations. Someone joining a Southern Baptist

church from the mid-west could find many cultural differences. Like joining a branch of your church that is a different part of the country, you notice that some of the things that were normal in your department may not even be practiced in this new branch or is considered not acceptable here. So given the time you are trying to adjust to the new rules really, you will experience some kind of conflict with the culture in this new place.

4. Ignore tensions: Ignoring the friction inside any team would kill the team's future growth. It is not always appropriate to see conflict as a negative. Stress can lead to positive growth in any organization if treated healthily. The Apostles took up the topic and hired others for assistance. This form of action demonstrates a real leader's character when coping with a crisis.

5. Lastly, jealousy, that vile green monster called jealousy can lead to the fall of great teams and congregations when people feel that the person who has it now does not deserve it as much as them. Or when they think they are better suited for a role in the church than whoever as chosen by the pastor, that can cause so much destruction as it spreads its roots into the hearts of people and very soon keeps the thought until it becomes full-blown hatred at this point all they want is to have the person removed and would go to any length to see that desire achieved.

How do we handle conflicts in our church?

Conflict in the church usually falls into three categories: conflict due to blatant sin among believers, conflict with leadership, the conflict between believers. Matthew 18:15-17 provides a straightforward procedure for the confrontation and restoration of a believer. Churches that lovingly discipline sinning individuals will curtail a great deal of conflict. Those who are frustrated should respect the leaders, be slow to accuse them, and speak the truth lovingly to them, not to others, Paul writes. The early church used the conflict to improve the ministry, acts 6:1-7 says, and the leaders took up complaints about a particular group. The church is not called to be judgmental of unbelievers, but it is expected to confront and restore those who are unrepentant of sins. Paul says the church should engage those who sin meekly and with the goal of restoration.

Conflict is best handled when individuals focus on loving others, with the intent of restoring relationships. Choose people who can help you resolve the dispute. If the first attempt does not accomplish the needed results, continue with another person or persons that can help with mediation. Remember that your goal is not to win an argument; it is to win your fellow believer in reconciliation.

To resolve conflicts, we must choose not to ignore problems. Nehemiah had many reasons for not getting involved. The dispute arose because of the nobles and officials. Good leadership understands the importance of not only getting involved but also resolving the conflict. We are often tempted to ignore or to overlook competition. It's straightforward to know about problems and, yet, give no attention to them. However, good leadership understands the importance of getting involved and resolving conflicts. We can't ignore problems; we must not just ignore them but instead address them. The bible says, "To resolve conflict, Godly Leaders Must Not Ignore Problems" The Bible described the response of the Israelites to their Jewish brothers when they learned they were in debt to pay taxes to Artaxerxes. The debt was so high that many of Israel's children had to be sold into slavery to pay the debt. These where the conflict was; it was between the poor and the nobles. The Israelites were angry at the Jews for the way they were paying the taxes to the king, but they couldn't find a solution.

Godly leaders must cultivate a Justified Indignation to overcome conflict. Rage is one part of being created in God's image. Jesus was wroth with sin and tried to bring redemption. We need holy indignation in our lives, our churches and our nations to correct the wrong. We should have anger over sin, not to cause trouble, but to help bring justice. God's righteous wrath should be inside every believer, he says. The Bible states Nehemiah was furious over the situation because he was serious about it. As many of us are, he was not apathetic, but rather enthusiastic about what needs to be done to address issues. He got agitated, and this is a sign that he's a man of rage.

Most anger that men struggle with is selfish anger instead of righteous anger. Righteous anger should be motivated by injustice towards God or others. When considering personal offence, righteous anger should respond differently. Jesus demonstrated righteous anger by turning over tables in the temple and by whipping a whip in John 2:14-16. Most anger is not anger about offence towards God, but because pride has been hurt or we have been treated unjustly. It says, "I deserve better than this." It is anger because our pride is broken, or our unjust treatment has been shown to us. It should be gentle in response to personal offence. It is the same anger Christ showed us in his example for us as we go through suffering.

To Resolve Conflict, Godly Leaders must be Patient and Self-controlled. Nehemiah took time to think about the situation and pondered it in his mind. Most people's anger and response are not calculated. Sometimes, it may even be wise to wait because the problem might work itself out. We need patience in changing the hearts of others, especially leaders, says Proverbs 25:15.

Seek wise counsel Nehemiah talked to himself and discerned how to respond to the situation. People who don't get counsel often make their situation worse. People make the wrong decisions for lack of good counsel. Who are the wise counsellors that you communicate with, especially in a potential conflict? How have they helped guide you in the past? The bible says, *"For lack of guidance a nation falls, but many advisers make victory sure"* The Bible advises us to be patient and to get good counsel, and to seek it from someone who has been through the same trials and tribulations as we have been through. The bible recommends seeking out a mentor and good counsel from someone you know and whom you feel comfortable talking to if you can't get it from anyone else.

Godly Leaders must Practice a Biblical Method of Confrontation to Resolve conflict. Jesus said that we should approach people one on one. Jesus also said that people should not tell everybody about sin without first speaking to the person in sin. If a person refuses to listen to a challenge, one or two others should take him or her to the church. If they still do not respond, they should be disciplined by the church, Jesus says. The church should punish those who refuse to listen or who spread rumors about others. It is crucial first to approach the person privately because there could be a misunderstanding. The person in question should be challenged personally because he or she may be struggling with sin and want help. The leader should challenge the leader privately to not spread rumors behind his or her back and harm a friend's back. The challenge should be private and should be carried out in front of the whole group, not just one person, as in the case of Nehemiah 5:7-9. It should be done in a public way so that people can see the leader's face and hear the truth.

Jesus taught that the second confrontation was to confirm the sin. Two or three witnesses was the minimum amount of witnesses needed to convict anyone of a crime. In Nehemiah's situation, the leaders' corruption was public; everybody knew about it. Paul said, "a little leaven leavens the whole lump" (1 Cor 5:6). Sin spreads rapidly and must be confronted in love with wisdom and discernment, he says. It should be done again with one or two more witnesses to confirm that it becomes a matter for the church if they don't respond. The leaders should be shunned and removed from the congregation until they repent, Paul says. The public confrontation will help others to fear God and turn from their sin, he adds. The bible says, "A little leaven leavening leavened the whole lumps", this is the key to stopping corruption from spreading quickly, Paul adds.

It's something that we rarely see happen in our churches, the bible says; nobody wants to rock the boat, so they say nothing.

One of the ways that Nehemiah challenged the nobles to repent was by the fear of the Lord. In Matthew 18:23-35, Peter asked Jesus how many times he should forgive someone, and Jesus replied, "No, seventy times seven" Christ motivated the disciples to forgive by the discipline of God, the Fear of God. Christ's sacrifice paid the eternal penalty for our times of unrighteous conflict, just as it did our other sins. But, if we don't forgive others, God will not forgive us (Matt 6:14). As Christ taught, he will often hand us over to torturers, to bring us to repentance (1 Cor 5:5) Paul commands the Corinthian church to hand an unrepentant man over to Satan (1 St. 5: 5). We also see God discipline King Saul, through a tormenting demon (1 Sam 16:14). He promised to send them to the torturers if they didn't forgive from the heart.

Conflict is a result of the fall. To be in discord is to be human. Peacemaker never means "ruffling feathers" or causing conflict. Amid this world of friction, Christ said: "Blessed are the peacemakers for they will be called sons of God" (Matthew 5:9) in describing those who are part of the kingdom of heaven, he said they would be known for working for peace and resolving discord. Nehemiah 5:1-13: How do godly leaders resolve conflict? How do we become the peacemaker that we have been called to be? 5:14-15: How can we become a Godly Leader? 6:15-16: How does one resolve conflict in the world of today? 7:17-9:

Accountability is a wise principle for battling all sins: lust, idolatry, anger, etc. Nehemiah established an accountability system amongst the priests and ultimately, before God as they took an oath. In the same way, we must find people who have integrity and wisdom to help counsel. We should seek godly accountability partners and invite them to speak into our lives or in the lives of those we are helping. Accountability is instead a fantastic way to grow spiritually as well as to resolve conflict resolution.

How can godly leaders be more effective in resolving conflict in their own lives and with others? To determine a dispute, Godly leaders must not ignore problems resolving conflict. Leaders must be patient and self-controlled. To resolve a conflict, Leaders must encourage the fear of the Lord and set an example. To help resolve a dispute in your life, use the leader by example, motto.

---- CHAPTER 6 ----

MY BROTHERS KEEPER: CARING FOR OTHERS

Nurturing Strength And Opportunities

This chapter, is a sequel to the previous chapter. Excellent conflict management in the organization draws on the strengths (Skills) of the leadership and the opportunities in the organization. Conflicts in the organization are not always negative, but have some positive impact on the organization as it helps the organization's leaders to discover talents. As seen in the case of Stephen and Philip (Acts 6:1-10).

Consequently, conflict resolution is an opportunity to identify your strengths and weaknesses. Nurturing these strengths and converting your weakness and threats to opportunities enhances your leadership qualities as a minister. Moreover, conflict resolution in any organization is a function of using strength to take advantage of the opportunities. However, you have to first discover your weaknesses and threats which are in essence, opportunities for development. When you nurture your opportunities, they become your areas of strength.

SWOT Analysis And Church Strategy

As you can see these discussions on strengths and opportunities invoke a consciousness of the management concept of SWOT analysis. The SWOT matrix is a management technique for strategic planning. It is frequently used in project planning, decision-making, or business competitiveness. It assists an individual or an organization that identifies their strengths, weaknesses, opportunities and threats.

SWOT analysis facilitates the decision-making process of the individual and corporate organization with, a defined objective. As a result, SWOT model is not limited to profit-seeking organizations. But, it can be simulated and adopted in any organization with specific goals. These organizations could be orphanages, public health centers, charity organizations, non-profit organizations, religious organizations (churches), academic institutions, government bodies, and individuals. SWOT analysis can also aid national decision-making, project planning, and execution.

SWOT analysis can be used in developing a strategy for the church. SWOT based Strategy involve using the accepted 2x2 matrix to model internal and external metrics of the church to decide and assess the most significant factors of the church with the potential to alter its objectives and to identify the relationships between these internal and external dynamics driving the church growth. For instance, a strong correlation between strengths and opportunities suggest excellent prospects for the use of constructive expansion strategy. Conversely, a strong relationship between weaknesses and threats could be interpreted as a potential warning requiring the use of a self-protective strategy.

Harmonizing And Adapting Strengths And Opportunities

The SWOT matrix helps to harmonize and adapt corresponding factors using the 2x2 matrix. On the one hand, it matches strengths to opportunities. On the other hand, it converts or adapts weaknesses or threats into opportunities or strengths. This brings us back to the title of this chapter "Nurturing – Strengths and Opportunities."

Nurturing Strengths And Opportunities In The Church

Although the SWOT model was originally designed as a management practice for business, it has been adapted and adopted in various settings including the church as a mechanism for nurturing strengths and opportunities to manage perceived organizational weaknesses and threats. In church leadership and development The SWOT matrix provides direction to the next stages of development. Nurturing, strengths and opportunities involve growing and matching strengths to opportunities in the church for leaders as individuals and the church as an organization. It helps to maximize the potentials of the human capacity and the organization's capabilities. Be that as it may, let's attempt to find a meaning for the word nurturing within the purview of church leadership.

I also like the SOAR analysis.

SOAR analysis is a strategic planning technique which helps organizations focus on their current strengths and opportunities, and create a vision of future aspirations and the result they will bring.

In contrast to SWOT analysis, the SOAR model uses appreciative inquiry to focus the organization on what is known to work, rather than internal weaknesses or perceived threats that might not eventuate.

The output from a SOAR analysis is a set of actions that leverage strengths and opportunities to strive for shared aspirations with measurable results. It provides a basis for further in-depth analysis using other strategic tools.

Nurturing As A Leadership Responsibility Is Caring For Others And Nourishing With The Word Of God

In the apostolic, nurture is an action word that connotes the impartation of anointing or power. It also refers to the process of providing, caring, and facilitating the spiritual, moral, and psychological development of the brethren.

As parents, we nurture the child to maturity. This is to provide for their necessities such as clothing, shelter, security, food, and looking after their wellbeing. Nurturing creates the opportunity to offer love and care. It is giving a person what they need. Likewise, in church leadership, nurturing carries the same definition and much more. To nurture means to teach, it also means discipleship. The apostolic office and pastoral office are two offices that have the responsibility of nurturing.

According to world health organization Nurturing care refers to a stable environment created by parents and other caregivers that ensures children's good health and nutrition, protects them from threats, and gives the child opportunities for early learning, through interactions that are emotionally supportive and responsive. Nurturing involves grooming. Spiritual nurturing comes about through ministering to people by caring, loving, empathizing, and being supportive. Jesus Christ groomed his disciples based on their strength and the opportunities that avail them in the ministry. He nurtured them as fishers of men (opportunity) by taking advantage of their skills as fishermen which were their strength (Matthew 4:19).

> Then He said to them, "Follow Me, and I will make you fishers of men." (Matthew 4:19)

In ministerial leadership, pastoral care involves nurturing care. Nurturing care in the church is like nurturing care in the nuclear family, where we respond to the need of the child from cradle to adolescence. Accordingly, Apostle Paul said:

> He is the one we proclaim, admonishing and teaching everyone with all wisdom, so that we may present everyone fully mature in Christ (Colossians 1:28 - NIV).

Admonishing and teaching in this context is synonymous with nurturing, rephrasing Apostle Paul's statement we have the following *"Nurturing everyone with all wisdom, so that we may present everyone fully mature in Christ."*

Essentially nurturing everyone refers to nurturing their strength and opportunities for kingdom purpose or ministerial responsibilities.

Ministerial or church leadership is critical to the growth of the church; hence, Jesus Christ, after he has nurtured his disciples quiz them about his identity.

> When Jesus came into the region of Caesarea Philippi, He asked His disciples, saying, "Who do men say that I, the Son of Man, am? "So they said, "Some say John the Baptist, some Elijah, and others Jeremiah or one of the prophets. "He said to them, "But who do you say that I am? "Simon Peter answered and said, "You are the Christ, the Son of the living God. "Jesus answered and said to him, "Blessed are you, Simon Bar-Jonah, for flesh and blood has not revealed this to you, but My Father who is in heaven. And I also say to you that you are Peter, and on this rock I will build My church, and the gates of Hades shall not prevail against it. And I will give you the keys of the kingdom of heaven, and whatever you bind on earth will be bound in heaven, and whatever you loose on earth will be loosed in heaven. "Then He commanded His disciples that they should tell no one that He was Jesus the Christ. (Matthew 16:13-20)

This event heralded the laying of the foundation of the Church and was the evidence of Jesus Christ, transferring his leadership and authority to Peter.

The definition of church leadership is maturity and accountability. As someone in church leadership, your responsibility in nurturing strengths and opportunities is first to build yourself to the maturity of Jesus Christ and be accountable. The second is to support your congregation in developing their potentials, thereby building the body of Christ. Thus, the fundamental question is

"How do I help my congregation (the spiritual child/children) develop his/her potential?"

Apostle Paul wrote, *"My little children, of whom I travail in birth again until Christ be formed in you,"* (Galatians 4:19).

Travail, in this context is like going through the labor process that precedes the birth of a child. By interpretation, the writer conveyed that he is consistently laboring to nurture the brethren until they come to the maturity of Jesus Christ. Christ forming in them points to developing, caring, and demonstrating the anointing and nature of Jesus Christ.

As church leaders, instead of seeing yourself as a hireling (John 10:12-15) you are the good shepherd (1st Peter 5:1-4) of the flock. The scriptures confirm this as seen here.

> The elders who are among you I exhort, I who am a fellow elder and a witness of the sufferings of Christ, and also a partaker of the glory that will be revealed: Shepherd the flock of God which is among you, serving as overseers, not by compulsion but willingly, not for dishonest gain but eagerly; nor as being lords over those entrusted to you, but being examples to the flock; and when the Chief Shepherd appears, you will receive the crown of glory that does not fade away. (1 Peter 5:1-4)

Nurturing help to identify and develop the (talents) strengths and opportunities in your church congregation and help to direct these strengths and opportunities for kingdom development and purpose. Recognize opportunities could be your weaknesses and threats. So, I have listed some strength and opportunities as pertain to the church. This list is not exhaustive and was not intended to be. But, it can serve as a guide. You can populate or increase the list as identified in your church or local assembly.

Church Strengths
- Congregation,
- Church workers
- Church volunteers
- Church board members
- Spiritual Gifts
- The Fruit of the Spirit
- All Types of Prayers
- Praying in the Holy Spirit
- Baptism of the Holy Ghost
- Praying in tongues
- The Apostle
- The Prophet
- The Evangelist
- The Teacher
- The Pastor
- The name of Jesus,
- The Blood of Jesus
- The word of God

- Soul-winning
- Fasting
- Church Address and location
- Church building
- Church equipment
- Church offerings
- Grants, funding, and partners
- Other sources of income
- Church Activities
- Church Management
- Church programs and systems
- Nurturing Experience
- Testimony
- Giving Thanks
- Giving

Opportunities

- Future trends in your ministerial practice
- Change in the culture of your local community
- The economy (local, national, or international)
- Funding sources (foundations, donors, partners)
- Changes (in the age, race, gender, and culture of local community)
- The physical location (is your church building in a developing and growing part of town? Are there connecting routes? Is it easy to connect with other communities from your location? What is the proximity of your church to the residence of your congregation?

- Are there bus routes or links in your church location or the nearest bus stop?
- Legislation (how does legislation affect your church? For instance, same-sex marriage)
- The population of unbelievers or unsaved souls

Your Strength As The Spiritual Leader

- The love of God (John 13:34)
- The Whole Armor of God (Ephesians 6:10-20)
- The Holy Spirit (Acts 1:8; John 14:13-26)
- Delegated power (Luke 10:19-20)
- The spiritual gifts (1 Corinthians 12:1-11)
- The Fruit of the Holy Spirit (Galatians 5:22-23)
- The name of Jesus Christ (Matthew 28:17-19)
- The blood of Jesus Christ (Revelation 12:11)
- Study the word consistently (2 Timothy 2:15)
- The word in you (Colossians 3:16-17)
- Consistent prayer life (1 Thessalonians 5:17)
- Rejoice always (1 Thessalonians 5:16)
- Give thanks (1 Thessalonians 5:18)
- Meditate upon the word day and night (Joshua 1:8)
- Finally take a course in church leadership.

Your Opportunities as a Spiritual Leader

There are several opportunities for you as a spiritual leader, some of these I have listed above. You can disciple the new brethren, be the church administrator, you can also function in any of the fivefold offices and many more. But, the greatest opportunity is to go out there on Soul Winning. Here are scriptural references mandating us leaders to be like Christ in this world (Acts 10:33-48; Matthew 9:35-38; Matthew 28:19-20; John 20:21).

Recognize that these lists are basic and not comprehensive; you can populate it depending on your individual preference and revelation. But, if nurture these strengths and opportunities, you will not fail in your ministry.

The easiest way to nurture your opportunities as the spiritual leader is to first identify and stir up your gifts (2 Timothy 1:6-7). This will guide you to the office where you will function.

Understand that the old saying, "opportunity comes but once" is a fallacy, opportunities never come, It is your gift that creates your opportunities. Recognizing your gifts and nurturing them opens to you a world of opportunities beyond your imagination.

> **A man's gift makes room for him, And brings him before great men (Proverbs 18:16-21)**

Though it can take years to nurture strengths and opportunities in the body of Christ, understanding your strengths and opportunities and that of the congregation is a rewarding church growth strategy. Once, you get it right, the rewards are remarkable.

How to Nurture Your Strength and Opportunities

What makes your congregation extraordinary? Have you identified your congregation's strengths and opportunities? Do you know how to nurture and inspire a creative congregation?

In a world full of stereotypes, as ministers of the gospel and leaders, we sometimes get caught up in what church activities we "think the congregation should be doing" rather than **activities for the congregation.**

How does that mega crusade or three-week summits pack full of delegates from every corner of the universe nourish or nurture your congregation? A malnourished congregation will not stand the test of time. The scriptures teach whatever you sow, that is what you will reap (Galatians 6:7). The measure you give is the measure you get (Luke 6:38). You may assume your activities attract great crowds but do it encourage or nurture your congregation's creative strengths?

Nurturing strength and opportunities change your congregation from spectators to disciples. Once the strengths and opportunities of your congregation are identified and groomed instead of depending on you, they depend on God. Instead of waiting for you to perform a miracle, they take the initiative to demonstrate the miracle. Instead of expecting miracles, they create miracles; instead of asking for prayers, they teach how to pray. You don't have to push them anymore, but they are pulled by their conviction. How often do church leaders burn-out or break-down as a result of pushing the congregation instead of allowing the Holy Spirit to pull or lead them (Romans 8:14)?

Each Member Of Your Congregation Is Special And Unique

As pastors and ministers of the gospel, it is your responsibility to nurture and discover your congregation's talents. Endless church programs and activities that engage your congregation may quickly bore and wear them out. If you have been in the church leadership position and have organized some church activities, you are most likely familiar with this. As a preacher, we must find the time to discover and identify what makes each member of the congregation unique and foster what makes them special.

How to Nurture Your Congregation's Strength in 3 Easy Steps

1. **Observe and identify your congregation's** strength. Every congregation has a combination of strengths and opportunities. As I stated above **each member of your congregation** is special and unique. Identify what this strength is for your church.

Observe what strength your congregation demonstrates. Look for ways to develop those strengths.

For instance, your congregation may be blessed with brethren who love to sing and dance. Develop a music training workshop where they can harness these aptitudes and avail them opportunities to demonstrate these strengths in your church programs. Provide learning opportunities and create engaging activities that foster love for music and praise worship. Your congregation will be more willing to learn when you provide the enabling environment and culture.

2. **Recognize the congregation's contributions.** Recognizing, approving, and rewarding your congregation's strengths are imperative not only for nurturing their strength but also for structuring their life and reinforcing their

confidence. Don't underestimate the power of words. Start by simply saying "thank you." It's important to verbalize the values regularly to the congregation, and there are many creative ideas to do so. Gather the volunteers from your church and read a poem of gratitude. Or you can create cards with inspirational bible verses about service or quotes about volunteering to uplift and celebrate your church congregation.

3. **Provide resources to nurture your congregation's strength.** Provide an appropriate and equipped learning environment based on your **congregation**'s interests.

What If I Don't Know My Congregation's Strengths?

Sometimes, it may be hard to identify our **congregation's** strengths, especially when the congregation is large. This shouldn't be an excuse to avoid your responsibility as a spiritual leader. By splitting the congregation into units call cell groups to facilitate easy group management. And facilitate one-on-one conversations. Offering diverse activities including art, sports, and observing how each group interacts with various activities can help you identify what their strengths are. In addition, you can network (team up) with other ministries or churches you deem have a similar vision.

Understand Your Strengths And Recognize Your Opportunities

Now you have to point the searchlight on yourself looking inward to know what exactly you are capable of doing. Understanding your strengths and that of your congregation will enhance your capacity to support their spiritual and secular development by nurturing their strength and opportunities.

Recognize in divine dictum there are no disadvantages but opportunities we see disadvantages when we cannot find the right teammate. Likewise, in Christian leadership, there are no weaknesses, because weaknesses, threats, and disadvantages are turned into opportunities as seen in these scriptures.

> Concerning this thing, I pleaded with the Lord three times that it might depart from me. And He said to me, "My grace is sufficient for you, for My strength is made perfect in weakness." Therefore most gladly I will rather boast in my infirmities, that the power of Christ may rest upon me. Therefore I take pleasure in infirmities, in reproaches, in needs, in persecutions, in distresses, for Christ's sake. For when I am weak, then I am strong (2nd Corinthians 12:8-10).

Moreover, our infirmities were taken away through the death, burial, and resurrection of Jesus Christ (Matthew 8:17). As a result, our weaknesses were redefined as opportunities for strength the moment we were baptized into the body of Christ (Romans 6:3-6; 1st Corinthians 12:12-27). Hence, Apostle Paul wrote I can do all things through Christ who strengthens me (Philippians 4:13).

In this usage "through Christ who strengthens me" stand for the empowerment through the anointing of the Holy Spirit and empowerment through cooperating with Jesus Christ as the head of the church. Cooperating with Jesus Christ as Christian leaders exposes you to divine resources and the wisdom of God. It helps you develop opportunities and strengths out of your weaknesses.

The Manifestation Of Gideon

> And there came an angel of the Lord, and sat under an oak which was in Ophrah, that pertained unto Joash the Abiezrite: and his son Gideon threshed wheat by the winepress, to hide it from the Midianites. And the angel of the Lord appeared unto him, and said unto him; The Lord is with thee, thou mighty man of valour. And Gideon said unto him, Oh my Lord, if the Lord be with us, why then is all this befallen us? And where be all his miracles which our fathers told us of, saying, Did not the Lord bring us up from Egypt? But now the Lord hath forsaken us, and delivered us into the hands of the Midianites. And the Lord looked upon him, and said, Go in this thy might, and thou shalt save Israel from the hand of the Midianites: have not I sent thee? And he said unto him, Oh my Lord, wherewith shall I save Israel? Behold, my family is poor in Manasseh, and I am the least in my father's house. And the Lord said unto him, Surely I will be with thee, and thou shalt smite the Midianites as one man (Judges 6:11-16)

As we conclude this chapter let us examine the calling of Gideon. Gideon was a man of strength and courage. However, he was hidden. Similarly, in the church and among your congregation lies the resources and opportunities you have been praying about. Only by revelation as a ministry leader will you discover this wealth buried in your congregation. It took an angel to discover Gideon. Angels are ministers and envoys of God. Though in our dispensation, they now minister to us the saints (Hebrews 1:14; Revelation 3 - AMPC). Thus, you may not see an angel giving you instructions but, the inner witness of the Holy Spirit operating in you through the word of knowledge and wisdom (1st Corinthians 12:8).

As highlighted earlier, nurturing as church leaders, involves discovery talents and creating an enabling environment for them to function. Did you know? That, there are great pastors, apostles, evangelist, teachers, and prophets among your congregation but, like, Gideon they are hidden. They think that because they are not on the board of the church or on the church's frontline activities, they are not relevant. The Gideon perception is familiar in every church setting particularly when the church founders have structured the church around their families. This explains why there are few stewards in the church. They cannot see a future beyond their status. Besides, the church leaders that are trained to discover them are busy with how to build a mega edifice instead of how to build the brethren or the spiritual man.

Nurturing involves discerning talents (strength). Gideon was discovered, inspired and convinced to pursue divine purpose. He was equipped for the task long before the assignment was handed over to him. Likewise, Stephen and Philip were discovered (Acts 6:1-8). How about Timothy? Although Timothy was of the Christian parenthood, he nonetheless, was naïve and timid in the matters of the kingdom. Apostle Paul wrote to him encouraging him to stir up the gifts (strengths) that were bestowed upon him (2nd Timothy 1:6-7).

The church workers you think you don't have are seating right before you in your church. Will you discover and nurture them?

―― CHAPTER 7 ――

A THREEFOLD CORD IS NOT QUICKLY BROKEN.

TEAMWORK AND COLLABORATION

Here is a brilliant illustration of the power of teamwork and collaboration.

Charles B. Tripp the armless man and Eli Bowen the legless man riding a tandem 1890s Photo source: blackandwt

This unique illustration of teamwork, collaboration, and the benefit of synergy epitomize creating opportunity (value) out of weakness. That is to say; you leverage your strengths to redefine your weakness and threats as opportunity, thereby creating value.

According to Wikipedia the Teamwork is the collaborative effort of a group to effectively and efficiently achieve a common purpose or to complete a task. This definition develops from the extensive framework of a team, which is a collection of mutually dependent individuals who collectively harmonize their effort to achieve a common objective.

Great leaders often pull their efforts and expertise together to form a synergy. This synergy is what we call teamwork. A team brings together varieties of skills, talents, and strength to create synergy. Thus, the collaborative teamwork is the combination of cooperative forces that results in a fruitful endeavor.

Understanding the value of teamwork and becoming an effective member of a team is imperative for leaders both in the secular, spiritual, and business setting. For the church to function as one body, teamwork and collaboration are sacrosanct.

Teamwork is a requirement for accomplishing difficult tasks and executing complex projects. It cut across all aspects of life, from marriage to, business, and to the church setting, it is crucial to the successful execution of any divine project. God in His sovereignty demonstrated the relevance of teamwork in the church when He said:

> "Let Us make man in Our image, according to Our likeness; let them have dominion over the fish of the sea, over the birds of the air, and over the cattle, over all the earth and over every creeping thing that creeps on the earth." So God created man in His own image; in the image of God He created him; male and female He created them." (Genesis 1:26-27)

"Let Us", *"Our image"* and *"Our likeness"* are the keywords that define teamwork in God's creation. By this, God Almighty provided a blueprint for the church to model in demonstrating and establishing the kingdom of God on earth through the preaching of the gospel. Another early biblical demonstration of teamwork and collaboration was when Jethro visited Moses. As seen in the following passage.

Jethro Visits Moses Recommends Task Delegation, Teamwork, and Collaboration

> The next day Moses took his seat to serve as judge for the people, and they stood around him from morning till evening. When his father-in-law saw all that Moses was doing for the people, he said, "What is this you are doing for the people? Why do you alone sit as judge, while all these people stand around you from morning till evening?" Moses answered him, "Because the people come to me to seek God's will. Whenever they have a dispute, it is brought to me, and I decide between the parties and inform them of God's decrees and instructions." Moses' father-in-law replied, "What you are doing is not good. You and these people who come to you will only wear

yourselves out. The work is too heavy for you; you cannot handle it alone. Listen now to me and I will give you some advice, and may God be with you. You must be the people's representative before God and bring their disputes to him. Teach them his decrees and instructions, and show them the way they are to live and how they are to behave. But select capable men from all the people—men who fear God, trustworthy men who hate dishonest gain—and appoint them as officials over thousands, hundreds, fifties and tens. Have them serve as judges for the people at all times, but have them bring every difficult case to you; the simple cases they can decide themselves. That will make your load lighter, because they will share it with you. If you do this and God so commands, you will be able to stand the strain, and all these people will go home satisfied." Moses listened to his father-in-law and did everything he said. He chose capable men from all Israel and made them leaders of the people, officials over thousands, hundreds, fifties and tens. They served as judges for the people at all times. The difficult cases they brought to Moses, but the simple ones they decided themselves (Exodus 18: 13 – 27).

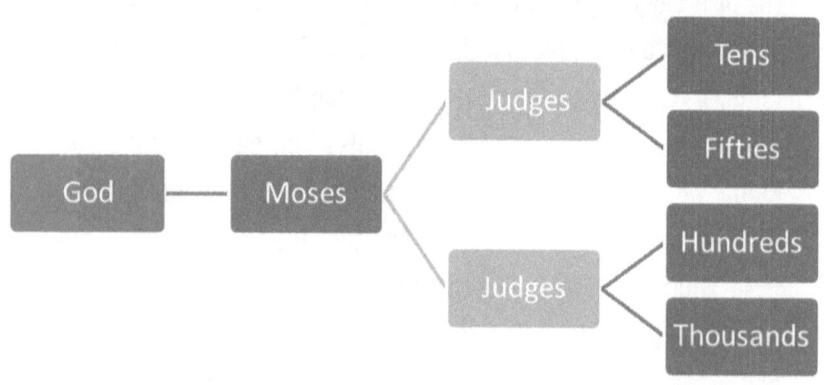

Jethro's Task Delegation, Teamwork, and Collaboration - Exodus 18: 13 – 27

The basic summary of this pictorial view is that Jethro's leadership approach was based on tasks delegation, teamwork, and collaboration. Recognize also that it was hierarchical, with God at the helm of affairs. Until Jethro visited Moses, Moses had no team, so, there was no tasks delegation, teamwork, and collaboration in executing the administrative tasks.

The Power Of Delegation, Teamwork, and Collaboration

Contrasting Moses leadership style and Jethro's leadership style (Exodus 18: 1 – 27)

Moses Leadership Style	Jethro's Leadership Style
Moses handled all cases	Moses handled only complex cases
No delegation	Tasks delegation, teamwork, and collaboration
Moses was sitting for over Twelve hours	Moses was sitting for fewer hours
Moses was wearing out	Moses was restored
Clients wait for a minimum of twelve hours.	Able to serve more clients
Waste of resources	Maximized resources
Clients were being worn out	The clients are not worn out
Poor efficiency and performance	Optimal efficiency and performance
Ineffective	Effective
Unhealthy	Healthy
Crude and unprofessional	Professional, creative and innovative
Poor time management	Advanced time management
Waste of talents	Talents identified and groomed

Teamwork As Divine Responsibility

God expects us to work together as a team. This was corroborated in the following scripture.

> I planted, Apollos watered, but God gave the increase. So then neither he who plants is anything, nor he who waters, but God who gives the increase. (1 Corinthians 3:6-7).

Teamwork as God intended it is not the same as the world view. Although the general understanding and delineation of teamwork are complementary, Christian teamwork, collaboration, and leadership are however defined with some variations. Church leadership and teamwork attract divine insight. Therefore, leadership in the body of Christ comes with divine empowerment. Though collaboration and collectivism as defining elements of the concept of teamwork are indispensable, christian teamwork, nonetheless, extends beyond collaboration and collectivism to incorporate stewardship, commitment, and accountability. Church leaders are ordained by God. So, they are accountable to God and not man.

Contrasting Teamwork as Spiritual and Temporal Leader

Whereas, teamwork as a spiritual leader is collaborating to develop people to the standard of God. In contrast, teamwork as a secular leader is developing structures to meet man's standard. This in itself constitutes a problem as a man cannot be a reliable standard. Consequently, leaders in corporate organization came up with policies defining the role of the leaders and leadership.

Though not measuring up to the standard of God and lack perfection, it was sufficient for the operations of corporate teamwork.

Secular teamwork is always headed by man coordinating to build the organization or achieve the strategic aims and objectives of the business. Spiritual teamwork on the contrary is about building lives, recreating lives, and raising an empire with God centered focus and purpose. Thus, in secular leadership, teamwork is planned according to the objectives of the organization. No organization can expand and remain competitive without the workforce coordinating as a team. Research, creativity, innovation, and development flourish when there is a synergy between leaders.

Having said that, spiritual teamwork is always headed by God Almighty. God has always been the active spiritual and temporal head of His people from creation. Nevertheless, the people rebelled in (1 Samuel 8:1-18) demanding for temporal leadership. Since then, God has always provided human headship or authority to represent Him in earthly affairs. Still, the office of spiritual leadership headed by the prophet has remained the same. Accordingly, church leaders are essentially God's wardens or stewards. This has been the precept since creation and validated by the following scriptures.

> And God has appointed these in the church: first apostles, second prophets, third teachers, after that miracles, then gifts of healings, helps, administrations, varieties of tongues. Are all apostles? Are all prophets? Are all teachers? Are all workers of miracles? Do all

> have gifts of healings? Do all speak with tongues? Do all interpret? (1 Corinthians 12:28-30).

Recognize that God made the appointment. Let us establish this fact by examining other scriptural illustrations.

> Having been built on the foundation of the apostles and prophets, Jesus Christ Himself being the chief cornerstone, in whom the whole building, being fitted together, grows into a holy temple in the Lord, 22 in whom you also are being built together for a dwelling place of God in the Spirit. (Ephesians 2:20-22)

The scriptures above reveal the teamwork between the apostles, the prophet, Jesus Christ, and God Almighty. In view of this revelation, it is therefore imperative to recognize as church leaders, your ultimate responsibility is building the body of Christ.

The Five fold Ministry Work As A Team

> And He Himself gave some to be apostles, some prophets, some evangelists, and some pastors and teachers, for the equipping of the saints for the work of ministry, for the edifying of the body of Christ, till we all come to the unity of the faith and of the knowledge of the Son of God, to a perfect man, to the measure of the stature of the fullness of Christ; that we should no longer be children, tossed to and fro and carried about with every wind of doctrine, by the trickery of men, in the cunning craftiness of deceitful plotting,

> but, speaking the truth in love, may grow up in all things into Him who is the head—Christ— from whom the whole body, joined and knit together by what every joint supply, according to the effective working by which every part does its share, causes growth of the body for the edifying of itself in love. (Ephesians 4:11-16).

The spiritual gifts were given to the church to enhance the operations and to accomplish tasks. But, did you realize that the spiritual gifts were linked to teamwork, collaboration, and leadership? We may not all be leaders but, we are all equipped to lead. And sooner or later, your chance to lead will come. This is fascinating when you examine the case of Stephen and Philip and other five teammates in (Acts 6). They were selected to serve tables as they were. But, God had other plans. The spiritual gifts distributed by the Holy Spirit were linked to leadership role in the church. They are the resource that would help the development of teamwork and collaboration in the body of Christ. As, a result, the spiritual gift functions best in teamwork.

The Relevance of the Holy Spirit in Teamwork

Having said that we can safely introduce the concept of divine or Christian teamwork. This is a construct that demonstrates teamwork in the body of Christ carries divine empowerment to accomplish God-given tasks. Accordingly, the scriptures read,

> "Behold, I send the Promise of My Father upon you; but tarry in the city of Jerusalem until you are endued with power from on high." (Luke 24:49)

> "But you shall receive power when the Holy Spirit has come upon you, and you shall be witnesses to Me in Jerusalem, and in all Judea and Samaria, and to the end of the earth." (Acts 1:8)

Teamwork is a function of the Holy Spirit. Without the enablement of the Holy Spirit, Christian leadership and teamwork will be disconcerting. Teamwork requires specialized skills to execute designated tasks. Without which the team cannot function. While the secular teamwork operates on secular skills and equipment, Christian teamwork operates by the Holy Spirit, His gifts and according to the various offices.

Fruit of the Spirit as Evidence Of Teamwork

The evidence of Christian teamwork is the fruit of the Spirit (Galatians 5:22-26). Details of the fruit of the Holy Spirit can be found here.

> But the fruit of the Spirit is love, joy, peace, longsuffering, kindness, goodness, faithfulness, gentleness, self-control. Against such there is no law. And those who are Christ's have crucified the flesh with its passions and desires. If we live in the Spirit, let us also walk in the Spirit. Let us not become conceited, provoking one another, envying one another. (Galatians 5:22-26)

> But also for this very reason, giving all diligence, add to your faith virtue, to virtue knowledge, to knowledge self-control, to self-control perseverance, to perseverance godliness to godliness brotherly kindness, and to brotherly kindness love. For, if these things are

yours and abound, you will be neither barren nor unfruitful in the knowledge of our Lord Jesus Christ. (2nd Peter 1:5-7)

The scriptures advocate the need to recognize that the leadership of the church must first function as a team as seen from the creation. We are all members of the body of Christ (Romans 12:4-5). Though we are individuals, unique, and different, yet we are part of the greater whole. When leaders work together as a team, they boost their energy getting much more done as a team. They are also beneficiaries of the value of having worked in unanimity, thus creating harmony in the church instead of disarray.

For as we have many members in one body, but all the members do not have the same function, so we, being many, are one body in Christ, and individually members of one another. (Romans 12:4-5)

The team works well when leaders observe certain dynamics that drive the functionality of a network. The church is an ecosystem, a network, of individuals in a team, and a network of teams. Teamwork does not necessarily mean acquiesces. There is a need to disagree when the disagreement is constructive. Teamwork starts with the contribution of each individual, as they pull their strengths together.

Each person working in a team has something unique and special to offer. So, we must recognize as church leaders, the diversity of resources that we manage through God's Grace and Love, together as a team we have options and vast benefits to share with one another.

Just as businesses, corporate organization, cultures, and nations of the world work with great minds, likewise, the church team has great players leading their team to high places. Teamwork depends on everyone recognizing her or his position and fulfilling it.

Teamwork also requires discipline, commitment, excellent communication, flexibility, and fluidity in approach. Your divine expectations as church leaders are designed within the framework of the love of Christ. That is, church leaders and church leadership demonstrate unreserved expectations in the power of God to help the teamwork. Teamwork is built upon a foundation of truth and love to achieve effectiveness, excellence, and efficiency.

The duty of the church leadership as a team is to emulate God's model. We should aspire to be more like God, so we can encourage others to seek the truth and love of God. Understand that Christian teamwork acknowledges God as the established authority and objective invisible team member of the church (Colossians 1:18 and Ephesians 5:23), responsible for strength and cohesion. Demonstrating love for God and love for one another, we facilitate the teamwork unity both in the home and in the body of Christ (Ephesians 4:13).

Love And Teamwork

Love is a function of teamwork, the bedrock of teamwork is mutual affection. Once we learn to love one another as Christ loved us (John 13:34-35), we demonstrate the binding force in a team is love. *A new commandment I give to you, that you love one another; as I have loved you, that you also love one another.*

By this all will know that you are My disciples, if you have love for one another (John 13:34-35).

Teamwork in One Body (the church)

> For as the body is one and has many members, but all the members of that one body, being many, are one body, so also is Christ. For by one Spirit we were all baptized into one body—whether Jews or Greeks, whether slaves or free—and have all been made to drink into one Spirit. For in fact the body is not one member but many. If the foot should say, "Because I am not a hand, I am not of the body," is it therefore not of the body? And if the ear should say, "Because I am not an eye, I am not of the body," is it therefore not of the body? If the whole body were an eye, where would be the hearing? If the whole were hearing, where would be the smelling? But now God has set the members, each one of them, in the body just as He pleased. And if they were all one member, where would the body be? (1st Corinthians 12:12-31).

The church, which is the body of Christ was designed to function as a team, as seen in the following scripture; we are many members but one body (Romans 12:4-5). Like our physical body where the body metabolism is determined by the effectual working in concert of the different organs to produce wellness and good health, the church (the body Jesus Christ) should do likewise. Just as the head is not the body, but part of the body, so is the minister or church leadership. The church is not the pastor and his family alone but supported by all of us. We are the church and one team in Jesus Christ. The church is strongest working together in one accord (Acts 1:14; Acts 2:46-47). Teamwork is the key to living life in harmony with God first and with our brethren so that we can do God's will.

Teamwork and Division of Task

There is task delegation in church leadership. The pastor is not the apostle. Neither is he the prophet, the evangelist or the teacher. He shouldn't be the treasurer or the church administrator. This was evident in Jethro's counsel to Moses (Exodus 18:1–27). Unfortunately, contemporary leadership still makes Moses mistake. Jesus Christ model of leadership had three inner squads, Peter, James, and John, his brother. Judas Iscariot though a thief, was in charge of the treasury (John 12:6).

THE CHURCH IS GOD'S INSTRUMENT OF MISSION

As the Body of Christ, the Church is responsible for the Great Commission. The primary physical expression of that universal body is the local church.

1. **Pattern of Ministry (Acts 2:41-47).**
2. **Helping Every Believer Discover Where They Fit**
   Every believer should discover their:
   S - Spiritual Gifts (I Corinthians 7:7).
   H - Heart/Passion (Philippians 2:13, Revelation 17:17).
   A - Abilities (Exodus 36:2).
   P - Personality (Psalm 139-:13-16).
   E - Experiences in Life (Romans 8:28).

(This list is referenced in The Purpose Driven Church, by Rick Warren).

God longs for every believer to be engaged in His global, Redemptive mission, and He has designed you, as a pastor or church leader, to help people discover their unique place of service!

Teamwork In Christ And Marriage

> Therefore a man shall leave his father and mother and be joined to his wife, and they shall become one flesh. (Genesis 2:24)

> For we are members of His body, of His flesh and of His bones. "For this reason a man shall leave his father and mother and be joined to his wife, and the two shall become one flesh." This is a great mystery, but I speak concerning Christ and the church. Nevertheless let each one of you in particular so love his own wife as himself, and let the wife see that she respects her husband. (Ephesians 5:30-33)

> For this reason a man shall leave his father and mother and be joined to his wife, and thetwo shall become one flesh." This is a great mystery, but I speak concerning Christ and the church. Nevertheless let each one of you in particular so love his own wife as himself, and let the wife see that she respects her husband. (Ephesians 5:31-33)

The scriptures above demonstrate the relevance of teamwork in the family and the church. After the teamwork that resulted in the creation of the universe (Genesis 1:26-27), God continues to demonstrate the need of teamwork in creating life when He introduced teamwork between Adam and Eve. Thus, introducing marriage as teamwork. Little wonder a lot of marriages fail because they lack the essential ingredients of teamwork. Apostle Paul in (Ephesians 5:32) discovered by revelation the plan of God right from creation was to present teamwork as the framework of the church introducing the functions of teamwork in the body of Jesus Christ (the church). The church setting as interpreted by Apostle Paul was developed like the family setting. It is to function like a close circuit where communication flows seamlessly and information transmitted without hitches.

Teamwork And Friendship

Apart from the family, another brilliant and familiar demonstration of teamwork is friendship. Friendship is the relationship between two or more individuals who chose to be friends. The element of choice is imperative in both friendship and teamwork. Teamwork is not about coercing people to achieve a task but the mutual concession to come together for a purpose. Friends support each other. Likewise, a team player supports the team. A friend isn't someone who always agrees with what you do, or say. But, someone that is willing to challenge you, to be the best you can be. In the same way, a team player encourages his fellow teammates to be their best.

Teamwork and Trinity

The first and oldest biblical evidence of teamwork is the Trinity demonstrated at the creation (Genesis 1:26-28). These scriptures revealed the Trinity: God the Father, Son, and Holy Spirit, collaborating as a team to create man. Furthermore, in

(Genesis 1:1–3), you will observe there were task distinction and definition among the Godhead. The individual member of the Godhead had a position to fill and a responsibility to accomplish in the creation of the world and man. Essentially tasks were delegated with authority to execute them. Recognize that God also created the man as a team (Genesis 1:26-27). The trinity is the most powerful, efficient, and effective teamwork existing today.

Finally, let's close this chapter with these brilliant scriptures on the power and value of teamwork.

> Two are better than one, because they have a good reward for their labor. For if they fall, one will lift up his companion. But woe to him who is alone when he falls, for he has no one to help him up. Again, if two lie down together, they will keep warm; But how can one be warm alone? Though one may be overpowered by another, two can withstand him. And a threefold cord is not quickly broken (Ecclesiastes 4:9–12).

CHAPTER 8

SELF-CARE AND STRESS MANAGEMENT:

Prosper and enjoy good health, as your soul also prospers.

> And He said to them, "Come aside by yourselves to a deserted place and rest a while." For there were many coming and going, and they did not even have time to eat (Mark 6:31- NKJV).

Church leadership even when well-planned can be disconcerting. This is because the church leader ministers not just to the local assembly, they also minister to the lost souls. They work 24/7/365 to meet the need of the world and the church. Even businesses have started to seek the support of church leaders for ideas, inspiration, and solutions.

The world is full of hurting men and women, the majority of young adults have lost hope in the future, and our boys and girls developing into adolescence have nothing to look up to, but, empty promises from the broken system. The welfare system has created the impression they can raise the balanced human being, such that at the slightest opportunities children are forcefully detached from their parents. These children eventually grow up in an atmosphere devoid of love and care of a loving parent called the care home. Jesus Christ saw this despondency among the populace when he said, "the harvest is plenty, but the laborers are few."

> Then Jesus went about all the cities and villages, teaching in their synagogues, preaching the gospel of the kingdom, and healing every sickness and every disease among the people. But when He saw the multitudes, He was moved with compassion for them, because they were weary and scattered, like sheep having no shepherd. Then He said to His disciples, "The harvest truly is plentiful, but the laborers are few. Therefore pray the Lord of the harvest to send out laborers into His harvest" (Matthew 9:35-38).

The best home to raise the balanced child is the church home or Christian home. As church leaders and ministers of God, we minister to our congregation, in the church house, at home, or in the workplace. As a result, the tendency to neglect self-care becomes likely. We understand the relevance of looking after ourselves. Often in our "busyness", we overlook self-care. We see it as insignificant and create excuses or reasons for busyness. The familiar examples of such excuses are that there is no time; it is not important; it is a waste of time, etc.

We forget that the growth and success of the ministry depend on the welfare (health, motivation, energy, and inspiration of the leadership). This is true not only for the church but for any corporate organization.

The theme of this chapter "Self-Care and Stress Management" is a combination of two independent concepts that are nonetheless correlated. This chapter shall define and explain these two concepts as well as discuss the correlation.

What is Self-Care?

> For no one ever hated his own body, but [instead] he nourishes and protects and cherishes it, just as Christ does the church (Ephesians 5:29).

As the scripture above suggests, self-care implies looking after one's own self. Self-care involves taking care of your bodies because without the body, you cannot function in your ministerial responsibilities. Though there are no direct scriptural references to self-care in the Holy Bible, the scriptures, however, teach the relevance of self-care, particularly for spiritual leaders. A brilliant scriptural demonstration of the significance of self-care in the ministry is illustrated as follows.

> Beloved, I wish above all things that thou mayest prosper and be in health, even as thy soul prospereth (3 John 2 - NKJV)

> Beloved, I pray that you may prosper in every way and [that your body] may keep well, even as [I know] your soul keeps well and prospers (3 John 2 - AMPC)

> Beloved, I pray that in every way you may succeed and prosper and be in good health [physically], just as [I know] your soul prospers [spiritually] (3 John 2 - AMP)

Recognize from these scriptures self-care involves your physical life (body) and spiritual life (Soul).

Self-care from scriptural teaching is a necessary requirement for individual spiritual development and church growth. Thus, God expects Christian leaders to invest in strengthening and caring for themselves fully. While we continue to give and minister to the church and the hurting world (Acts 6:1-6; 3 John 2), it is essential that we always ensure our readiness to give by looking after ourselves because we have nothing to give when we are empty. Investing in self-care (our body, mind, and spirit), will inspire us, energize, and rekindle our enthusiasm to serve God and minister to the world and the church successfully (Joshua 1:8).

What is Stress Management?

We shall briefly state what stress management is. Further discussions on the concept of stress management can be found in the conclusion of this chapter. Stress management, according to Wikipedia, is a range of activities, actions, procedures, and therapies intended at controlling an individual's level of stress.

Usually, the purpose is to enhance the health and wellbeing of the individual. As you may know, there are numerous occurrences in life that causes stress. Life can be stressful, especially when you are not saved. All these are referred to as stressors. Stress can have negative or positive effects on an individual. In this book, 'stress' refers only to a stress with undesirable consequences. Consequently, it is fair to say self-care is the process of preventing stress and improving your hearth as Christian leaders. Having said that, the problem with self-care is that there are too many enemies, activities, ideologies, mindset, or things that prevent self-care.

Here Are The Three Enemies Of Self-Care

1. Toiling and Busyness in Ministry

According to the King James Bible version dictionary, "toiling means to labor, work, and exert strength with pain and fatigue of body or mind, particularly of the body, with efforts of some continuance or duration". Other definitions from the internet are; "to labor continuously or work strenuously, to proceed with difficulty, exhausting labor or effort, and to work extremely hard". While there are various meaning to the word toiling, the meaning of toiling, as stated above, is sufficient for this discussion. But, the word toiling is not very popular in modern-day expressions. So, what is the closest word that explains toiling in the ministry? In my search, I discovered the word "Busyness". "Busyness" is very common in our daily lives and very popular with CEOs, Church leaders, ministers, employers, employees, professionals, and entrepreneurs.

Searching for the meaning of "busyness," I noticed that different industries have their way of explaining the word "busyness;" some call it, work overload, utilization, task saturation, etc. Many see it as busy. Whereas we may accept the other explanations of "busyness," in my experience as a minister and church leader, it not very accurate to say busyness is being busy. This meaning oversimplifies the activities involved in busyness. "Busyness" is working non-stop, work overload, task overload, activities overload, and job overload. (Were "over" here means excess, or over the board).

"Busyness" can also mean overcrowded lifestyle. In my personal assessment as a minister of the gospel and as an entrepreneur, it is when your effort is very high, and the output is very low or tends to zero. This means low productivity and decreased efficiency for the Christian leader. This is often the cause of conflicts and crisis in the organization and has been known to be responsible for conflict and crisis in the church as well. Workplace issues like increased employee turnover, increased absenteeism, increased lateness, distraction, anxiety, stress, and numerous sicknesses are some of the attributes of "busyness."

2. Your Environment

The place of the environment in self-care is paramount; it doesn't matter whether you agree or not, a good deal of credible research has identified your environment (whether church, home, or the workplace, even the gym and shopping malls), is crucial to your personal and spiritual growth and can influence your mood, and decisions. Your physical location determines your feelings in one of the following ways. Stressed, overwhelmed, relaxed, and confident?), the scriptures says "do not be deceived, Evil company corrupts good habits." (1st Corinthians 15:33) and two cannot walk together unless they agreed (Amos 3:3) the people you share your life and space with (your family, friends, colleagues, neighbors), contribute to your happiness and well-being in this space. If your environment is challenging, distracting or negative, consider changing it. Recognize Jesus Christ's statement:

> "Come aside by yourselves to a deserted place and rest a while." For there were many coming and going, and they did not even have time to eat (Mark 6:31- NKJV)

From the scriptures, you will realize that Jesus Christ had a habit of retiring into quite places, most of these places where retreats or recreations for him (Luke 5:16; Mark 1:35-39).

3. Procrastination - Delay

Procrastination is a thief of time, and the scripture says:

> He who observes the wind will not sow, and he who regards the clouds will not reap. As you do not know what the way of the wind is, Or how the bones grow in the womb of her who is with child, So you do not know the works of God who makes everything. In the morning sow your seed, And in the evening do not withhold your hand; For you do not know which will prosper, Either this or that, Or whether both alike will be good. (Ecclesiastes 11:4-6).

One of the lies we were sold is "no time", there is not enough time becomes real when you fail to place God first. When you often use the cliché 'I don't have the time' more often than not, your life is overcrowded. You are a client to "busyness" and living with the enemy called 'no time'. When you cannot find time for yourself in any activity in life, you have essentially become a slave to that activity. Likewise, as leaders in the establishment, if you do not have time for yourself, you are no longer an asset to that organization but, a security risk. That is, you are an accident waiting to happen. You must create time for yourself as leaders and the scriptures corroborate this in (Ecclesiastes 3:1-8).

According to Brendon Burchard author of high-performance habit, "Most people awake with a dream in their mind, but they let that dream die in the daylight". The dream dies because it was not acted upon. The Acts of the Apostles was written because the apostles acted. Delay becomes your enemy when you always reschedule your self-care need. When you delay your car's care (maintenance), you get the ticket or the car develops a fault and breakdown. Likewise, when, you delay your self-care as leaders, you burnout and eventually breakdown. Delay is dangerous because when you don't act on your dream, it dies.

> **Don't be trapped. Who, when, and what are you waiting for? When are you going to book that vacation you have always wanted?**

The Relevance Of Self-Care to a Church Leader

The majority of church leaders toils and suffers exhaustion in the ministry because they lack self-care. They think without their presence, the ministry will not grow. In fairness to them, they sincerely have a zeal for God. However, as recorded by Apostle Paul out of imprudence, they neglect the weighty matters of the kingdom pursuing their own interest.

> For I bear them witness that they have a zeal for God, but not according to knowledge. For they being ignorant of God's righteousness, and seeking to establish their own righteousness, have not submitted to the righteousness of God. For Christ is the end of the law for righteousness to everyone who believes (Romans10:2-4)

As church leaders, you must recognize the flock (church) is not yours but, Gods. You may be the pastor - spiritual father (1st Corinthians 4:15). Still, the congregation belongs to God. God is their ultimate father (Matthew 6:9-13; Matthew 23:9). As a result, it is the responsibility of God to build the church as seen in these two scriptures;

> I will build My church, and the gates of Hades shall not prevail against it. And I will give you the keys of the kingdom of heaven, and whatever you bind on earth will be bound in heaven, and whatever you loose on earth will be loosed in heaven." (Matthew 16:18-19)

> I planted, Apollos watered, but God gave the increase. So then neither he who plants is anything, nor he who waters, but God who gives the increase (1st Corinthians 3:6-7).

Practicing Self-care as a church leader prevents "busyness" and toiling in ministry, as it facilitates the serene atmosphere for inspiration, information, hearing seamless fellowship, and communication with God. So many church leaders have given up on their calling and ministry. Some abandoned their family because of the ministry and ended up losing everything. These people suffered because they neglected self-care. To avoid "busyness" or toiling in the ministry, let's look at some steps to self-care.

Steps To Self-Care To Avoid Toiling - "Busyness" - As A Church Leader

1. Develop A Scale Of Preference For Every Task

Identify and arrange your tasks in order of importance. In His creation plan, God had his daily activities planned out for six days and on the seventh day rested (Genesis 1-2). The Use of Gantt charts, time analysis or network flow will help to pinpoint and visualize your critical tasks. To identify your tasks, the Christian leader requires an open and objective mind. Because your decisions should be based on the value, they bring and not on the perceived emotional benefit. The value will create an atmosphere where you will wait on God for your essential decisions.

"Busyness" often eliminates the need to wait on God. It is driven by fear and lack of faith in God. It is a concept based on the more or harder I work, the more I can achieve. Efficiency and effectiveness in the ministry are not the results of hard work but of SMART (Specific, Measurable, Achievable, Realistic, Time-Bound) work. "Busyness" is working without a plan.

Continuous work does not allow time for review and revisions. Peter and his team toiled overnight fishing for fish, but they caught NOTHING (Luke 5:1-7). That is about twelve hours of ZERO Return on Investment (ROI). Now if you run your ministry or business on zero ROI every twelve hours in twelve years, you will still have zero ROI. That means your ministry will be shut down or you are out of business.

2. Create Time for God in your ministry

Creating time for God in your ministry allows God to use your ministry and positions you to receive divine ideas. In (Luke 5:1-7) Peter demonstrated what I described as allowing God to use your ministry for His outreaches, not your own mega crusades. Jesus Christ asked Peters for his boat, so, he could seat and address the audience. (Boat in this context could be your pulpit or entire ministry). When he finished speaking, he instructed Peter to launch out into the deep. This was a specific instruction "launch out into the deep." Your ministry may have closed just as Peter has closed his and was washing his nets at the shore. God is saying to you right now use your ministry to glorify me and go into the deep. Like Peter, you will have three thousand added to your church daily (Acts 2:41-42).

What you need for success as a leader or in your ministry is the right information. That information is with somebody. Ask God to inspire you. But, recognize, only in the place of self-care (sobriety will you assess the information).

Peter, who had no single fish (soul) in the last twelve hours by obeying the instructions from Jesus Christ gained so much that he needed help to manage his congregation.

3. Choice

The first of the steps to Self-Care to Avoid Toiling - "Busyness" - as a Church Leader was to develop a workable scale of preferences for your ministerial tasks. But, to develop a reliable and workable scale of preference for your ministerial duties, you need to know how to make the right choices. Choices are made every second, and even as you read this book, you made a choice, and you are making choices as you continue to read. After reading, you will also make a choice. As the writer of this book, I am making choices in the process of writing. The problem with choices is that ninety-nine per cent (99%) of the time, our choices are wrong. For instance, in the ministry, business, or life, the choice of "busyness" is counterproductive. God with all His supernatural abilities and prowess after His six days creation rested on the seventh day. So, toiling or the so-called hard work is not necessarily a sound business or management theory neither is it a scriptural principle. To be precise toiling was introduced as the result of the wrong choice of Adam and Eve (Genesis 3).

A good model of the scriptural understanding of choices is the Mary and Martha illustration.

> Now it came to pass, as they went, that he entered into a certain village: and a certain woman named Martha received him into her house. And she had a sister called Mary, which also sat at Jesus' feet, and heard his word. But Martha was cumbered about much serving, and came to him, and said, Lord, dose thou not care that my sister hath left me to serve alone? Bid her therefore that she

> helps me. And Jesus answered and said unto her, Martha, Martha; thou art careful and troubled about many things. But one thing is needful: and Mary hath chosen that good part, which shall not be taken away from her (Luke 10:38-42)

Observe that Martha was a victim of "busyness", that is, her life was overcrowded (Luke 10:41-42). Martha was busy with how to entertain Jesus Christ and make him comfortable, which was the traditional thing to do when you have guests. But, her sister Mary was listening to Jesus Christ teaching. Martha was not wrong in her choice, and Mary was not wrong either. When Martha saw that the chores were overwhelming, she needed Mary's support. In fact, Martha coming to Jesus Christ suggests that in her opinion, Mary was, wrong to seat listening to Jesus Christ while she was left alone with the services. Making the right choices is critical to a successful ministry or career. Your choice may not be, wrong, like Martha and Mary. The question Christian leaders should ask is whether their choice is appropriate.

Starting from Adam and Eve (Genesis 3), the Bible is full of men and women whose destiny would have shaken the world. Then, they made the wrong choice that ended their careers. The sequence progressed till present-day. Here are two familiar examples. King Saul lost the throne because he made the wrong choice to offer the sacrifice meant for the priest (1st Samuel13: 7-14) David's choice of not going to war when he should have gone was the start of his career fall (2nd Samuel 11: 1 - 2).

4. Change Your Perception Of Time-Work-Productivity Ratio

> Except the Lord build the house, they labor in vain that build it: except the Lord keep the city, the watchman wakes but in vain. It is vain for you to rise up early, to sit up late, to eat the bread of sorrows: for so he gives his beloved sleep... (Psalm 127: 1-2).

You or your ministry will not grow more than your energy allows. For supernatural growth in your ministry, you need God as confirmed by the psalmist above. The economic problem of scarcity of resources, the two ends meet, resource maximization and optimization has not only increased poverty but reduced the quality of life we live. The time-work-productivity ratio assessment over time has become a habit for most labor experts and Christian leaders. They argue the amount of work and time put into a task determines the output. Productivity is high when you put in more time and work harder. Well, not anymore. Because the law of diminishing returns has since set in and what we have today is reverse productivity.

With every extra hour more than what is required for any task is loss of efficiency. "Busyness" has also been attributed not only to ministers competing to have the largest auditorium, church, congregation, and finance. But, church leaders and workers also overworked themselves in the hope of recognition. Church leaders find themselves trapped in the cycle of "busyness" because of the endless bills they have to pay. As a result, they burden the congregation with emphasis on giving and sowing of seed. They create more wealth by creating ways to take more from the workers, such as pastor's birthday, pastor's gift day etc.

So, the natural tendency is "busyness" - to work, work, and work without rest. Not considering the adverse effect of overwork on health, social life, family life, and the overall ministry or business performance. If the Christian leader can trust God in managing the Church or business, there will be less toiling and "busyness." Business (SMEs and Startups) failures will reduce, suicide rate will reduce, divorces rates will reduced and marital challenges will reduce. Family cohesion and business will be fostered. Then, your ministry or business will perform well.

Thoughts dwelling on how to manage a successful ministry should not be allowed to persist. Because as Christian leaders you know the church or business idea was not yours in the first place. The owner of the church or business will always look after the church – (His body) or your business. But you as the steward have to position yourself in obedience to allow God to help you; this is why you need self-care to hear clearly when God speaks. Your best efforts are woefully insufficient to produce the results you desire to see in your ministry. Remember in (Genesis 3), Adam and Eve were naked and have no idea how to cover their nakedness. So, they use fig leaves as aprons to cover their nakedness and went into hiding.

> **And the eyes of them both were opened, and they knew that they were naked; and they sewed fig leaves together, and made themselves aprons (Genesis 3:7).**

But we know that God gave them a permanent and durable animal skin clothing to cover their nakedness.

> Unto Adam also and to his wife did the Lord God make coats of skins, and clothed them (Genesis 3:21).

God Is Not In Your Overcrowded Lifestyle

When you practice self-care, God will have your listening heart, and He will provide much more than you can imagine (Ephesians 3:20). Why join team "busyness" or "toiling"? Recognize you will not find God or hear His voice in the hustles and bustles of life. God didn't speak to Elijah from the storms, thunder, or tumultuous sky, Elijah heard God in the sound of gentle stillness (1st Kings 19:11-13).

And He said, Go out and stand on the mount before the Lord. And behold, the Lord passed by, and a great and strong wind rent the mountains and broke in pieces the rocks before the Lord, but the Lord was not in the wind; and after the wind an earthquake, but the Lord was not in the earthquake;

And after the earthquake a fire, but the Lord was not in the fire; and after the fire [a sound of gentle stillness and] a still, small voice.

> When Elijah heard the voice, he wrapped his face in his mantle and went out and stood in the entrance of the cave. And behold, there came a voice to him and said, What are you doing here, Elijah? (1 Kings 19:11-13 AMPC).

Self-care, Fasting and Dieting (1 Corinthians 10:31; Romans 14:17)

Spiritual growth and excellent spirit are the results of the correct diet rations. One of the greatest problems of weight loss is diet. Likewise, self-care includes the appropriate diet. There is the need for discipline when it comes to what you consume as Christian leaders. Controlling the urge for those favorite delicacies and cuisine are essential because Satan can use them to rob you of your glorious destiny. Eve and Adam (Genesis 3) lost their glorious estate because they had no control over their taste buds. Esau lost his birthright and inheritance for a pot of stew (Genesis 25:29-34). Satan tried the same trick on Daniel (Daniel 1:8-15) and Jesus Christ (Matthew 4:1-11) but failed.

There is a connection between spiritual leadership and food else. Satan wouldn't use the desire for food to snare Eve, Adam, and Esau. Jesus Christ and Daniel saw it and disapproved of it. It is of no use engaging in self-care and at the same time careless about your feeding habit. There is no wisdom in consuming all manner of junk food and spending the rest of your life in the gym losing weight. God's plan for His ministers and the church leaders includes a healthy diet and feeding habit. Daniel and the three Hebrew youths in (Daniel 1:11-21) lived on the vegetable menu for about two weeks, and they were better and had good health than those who fed on the king's menu. Our lifestyle is a reflection of our diet, and the food we eat tells a lot about who we are.

Rest or Vacation (Genesis 2:2-3)

Set a date for your vacation. The final point on steps to self-care to avoid toiling – "busyness" as a church leader, is setting a date or time for rest, always have vacation plan as a church leader. Vacation may not be feasible immediately if the ministry is just budding, at the very least you can take a day or two of rest. God worked for six days and rested for a day. Twenty-four days' work nonstop will require four days of rest. Whether in the church or business, there is a need to include vacation on your leadership plan. There are blessings attached to the day of rest. Note the two occasions God blessed in His creation were the creation of man and the seventh day He rested. This is to say if you plan your ministry or business and submit the plan to God, you operate the blessings of God.

Your ministry, business, vacations are already blessed. Every Christian leader should have a vacation included in their leadership curriculum, church growth, and personal development strategy, no matter how short. God's rest or vacation after six days of work was one day. In this analysis, you will notice that God worked more days than the average employees. On average, employees work from Monday to Friday that is five days rested on Saturday and Sunday, with this assessment, employees work five days and rest for two days. That translates to 12 days of rest for a month or 30 days' work. That is for every month your employee works for 18 days and rest for 12 days. However, church leaders, entrepreneurs, or business owners on average work throughout the week. This should be discouraged and discontinued. The number of wasted hours does not count towards the success and efficiency of your business.

Christian Leadership And Stress

To conclude this chapter, we shall examine stress management and church leadership. What is stress? Stress is how the body responds to changes in life; this includes "busyness". In most cases, stress is a mental activity that affects the body, health, and well-being. Life by nature is dynamic and involves consistent transformation on a daily basis. These changes could be spontaneous, revolutionary, dramatic, subtle, or aggressive. Accordingly, Wikipedia defined stress to mean harmful stress or distress. Every human being experience stress, but, it is more intricate once you are in a leadership role. It is impossible to avoid stress once you are a leader.

Causes Of Stress - Stressors

Factors responsible for stress in the ministry or church can be external or internal. Whereas external sources of stress arise from the external environment, internal stressors are mostly personal. Here are some familiar examples of stressors:

> Neglect (Acts 6:1-6): Neglect comes in type. It could neglect family responsibility, church responsibilities, neglect of financial responsibilities, neglect of marital responsibilities, neglecting your home, family, spouse, and children in the name of church leadership, just to mention a few. Others are the demand of your congregation (1 Samuel 8), wrong leadership style (Moses

- exodus 18:13-18), combining church leadership and work. Lack of finance, divorce, and dishonesty are also known to cause stress.

Stress Management

Stress management does not advocate zero stress, neither is it intended to completely eliminate stress but, to eliminate unwanted or unjustifiable stress often referred to as distress, as we know the pressure at work or anxiety over an event are forms of stress that can be harnessed using strengths and opportunities for fruitful outcomes. As a result, stress management seeks to effectively manage unavoidable stress. With the following scriptures pointing to stress management, I close this chapter.

> "Therefore I say to you, do not worry about your life, what you will eat or what you will drink; nor about your body, what you will put on. Is not life more than food and the body more than clothing? Look at the birds of the air, for they neither sow nor reap nor gather into barns; yet your heavenly Father feeds them. Are you not of more value than they? Which of you by worrying can add one cubit to his stature? "So why do you worry about clothing? Consider the lilies of the field, how they grow: they neither toil nor spin; and yet I say to you that even Solomon in all his glory was not arrayed like one of these. Now if God so clothes the grass of the field, which today is, and tomorrow is thrown into the oven, will He not much more clothe you, O you of little faith? "Therefore do not worry, saying, 'What shall we eat?' or 'What shall we drink?' or 'What shall we wear?' 'For after all these things the Gentiles seek. For your heavenly Father

knows that you need all these things. But, seek first the kingdom of God and His righteousness, and all these things shall be added to you.34 Therefore do not worry about tomorrow, for tomorrow will worry about its own things. Sufficient for the day is its own trouble (Matthew 6:25-34).

Similarly, Apostle Paul in Philippians wrote the following;

Be careful for nothing; but in everything by prayer and supplication with thanksgiving let your requests be made known unto God. And the peace of God, which passeth all understanding, shall keep your hearts and minds through Christ Jesus. Finally, brethren, whatsoever things are true, whatsoever things are honest, whatsoever things are just, whatsoever things are pure, whatsoever things are lovely, whatsoever things are of good report; if there be any virtue, and if there be any praise, think on these things. (Philippians 4:6-8)

Recognize the scriptures as seen above, introduce occupying your mind with the right thoughts. The word "careful" used in the context is the same as worry or anxiety.

Stress management strategies in the church differ from stress management approach in the circular world. So, know that self-care is one of the fundamental principles to stress management. Self-care help leaders avoid decision, activities, and plans that fuel stress and prevent crises in the church, ministry, family, home, or business. Beside self-care, here are other relevant antidotes to stress:

- Love
- Forgiveness
- Faith in God
- Believe God
- Perseverance
- Regular Bible study and meditating upon the Word of God (Joshua 1:8)
- Praying without ceasing
- Praying in the Holy Ghost
- Praying in tongues
- Connecting with other ministers
- Sports, hobbies, and having fun
- Seeking the support of health experts

─── CHAPTER 9 ───

Conclusion

The end of a thing is better than the beginning
In finishing this book, I like to emphasize God centered leadership as the foundation of church growth and success in the ministry. Beginning from creation, the unique nature of God's leadership was exemplified. Christian leaders are human representatives of God's divine order in the affairs of men. They hear from God directly and work with the inspiration of the Holy Spirit to ensure the purpose of God is established on earth. They introduce heavens rules into the affairs of men "Your kingdom come, Your will be done on earth as it is in heaven." (Matthew 6:10).

Biblical Leadership From Adam
In the creation, the leadership responsibility of the whole world was handed to Adam and Eve by God (Genesis 1:28). Like Esau (Genesis 25:29-34), Adam and Eve inadvertently lost this enviable position to Satan because they did not understand the

spiritual value of the authority bestowed on them. They did not understand the consequences of losing this position as the head of God's creation either. Noah and his family came next and were followed by the era of the tower of Babel (Genesis 11:1-9) where the people had one language (one voice and a common goal).

Abraham was the first spiritual leader and prophet of God demonstrated in the Book of Genesis after Abraham, came Moses in the books of Exodus to Deuteronomy. Moses leadership was seconded by Aaron and Levi as priests. This made Moses the administrative leader. Although the account of Moses was recorded up to Deuteronomy Moses leadership ended abruptly in the books of Numbers as a result of disobedience.

Joshua, an extension of Moses leadership, took over from Moses and closed Moses period of influence in the book of Joshua. Joshua era heralded the reign of judges a period when God used both male and female magistrates. The judges heralded Ruth's testimony that ushered in the leadership of Samuel, the priest, and the period when God used kings as administrative heads starting with King Saul and King David. This episode covered the books of Samuel to 2nd Chronicles. The priesthood of Ezra, Nehemiah, Esther, and the revelation of Job followed.

The leadership of the prophets from Isaiah to Malachi commenced and culminated in the coming of Jesus Christ. After the death and, the resurrection of Jesus Christ, the leadership of Peter and the other disciples including Stephen and Philip commenced with Apostle Paul introducing the leadership from the platform of Grace after his conversion (Acts 9:1-22). The leadership of Apostle Paul overshadowed that of Peter, and his account continued throughout the books of Romans to Hebrew. The accounts of biblical figures in leadership role ended in James, Peter, John, and Jude's books. Perhaps, John, because, of the book of revelation. It is interesting to note these leaders had one thing in common. They were all chosen and inspired by God.

An interesting scriptural illustration of the relevance of church leadership to the body of Christ is the call of Joshua.

> Be strong and of good courage, for to this people you shall divide as an inheritance the land which I swore to their fathers to give them. (Joshua 1:6).

Observe Joshua was to dispense the promises of God, which they inherited to the congregation. Similarly, in the church, the body of Christ, church leaders are deputies of God responsible for the distribution of God's abundant love and mercy to his flock. They interpret and transmit the messages and blessings of God through Jesus Christ to the church. Hence, Church Leadership, in summary, is Influencing and serving others to discover and fulfil their purpose in God

Obedience The Key To Sustaining Leadership

Obedience is the key to sustaining divine leadership. Moses lost his leadership role because; he disobeyed God. He could not discern what God's intention was when God asked him to speak to the rock. Even without discerning, he could have followed the instructions he received from God. Christian leadership comes with such a huge responsibility that demands the minister connects with the Holy Spirit to be empowered to execute God's instructions. Hence, obedience is central to the success of Christian leaders. It is obvious from the scriptures Adam, Eve, Moses, and King Saul received divine instruction. But, choose to do otherwise. Moses's circumstance was nonetheless instructive as reveal by Apostle Paul.

God Desires for ALL the People in the World to KNOW Him through Jesus Christ.

1. Old Testament Illustrations

"I will bless those who bless you, and whoever curses you I will curse, and all peoples on earth will be blessed through you." (Genesis 12:3)

"... so that all the peoples of the earth may know that the Lord is God and that there is no other." (I Kings 8:60)

"May God be gracious to us and bless us that your ways may be known on earth, your salvation among all nations." (Psalm 67:1-2)

2. New Testament Illustrations

"But the angel said to them, 'Do not be afraid. I bring you good news of great joy that will be for all the people. Today in the town of David a Savior has been born to you; He is Christ the Lord." (Luke 2:10)

"Therefore go and make disciples of all nations ..." (Matthew 28:18)

"... so that all nations might believe and obey Him." (Romans 16:26b)

"He is the atoning sacrifice for our sins, and not only for ours but also for the sins of the whole world." (1John 2:2)

Moses, the Rock, and the Water
The Event At Horeb

> Then all the congregation of the children of Israel set out on their journey from the Wilderness of Sin, according to the commandment of the LORD, and camped in Rephidim; but there was no water for the people to drink. Therefore the people contended with Moses, and said, "Give us water that we may drink." So Moses said to them, "Why do you contend with me? Why do you tempt the LORD?" And the people thirsted there for water, and the people complained against Moses, and said, "Why is it you have brought us up out of Egypt, to kill us and our children and our livestock with thirst?" So Moses cried out to the LORD, saying, "What shall I do with this people? They are almost ready to stone me!" And the LORD said to Moses, "Go on before the people, and take with you some of the elders of Israel. Also take in your hand your rod with which you struck the river, and go.Behold, I will stand before you there on the rock in Horeb; and you shall strike the rock, and water will come out of it, that the people may drink."And Moses did so in the sight of the elders of Israel. (Exodus 17:1-6)

The Event At Kadesh

> Now there was no water for the congregation; so they gathered together against Moses and Aaron. And the people contended with Moses and spoke, saying: "If only we had died when our brethren died before the LORD! Why have you brought up the assembly of the LORD into this wilderness, that we and our animals should die here? And why have you made us come up out of Egypt, to bring us to this evil place? It is not a place of grain or figs or vines or pomegranates; nor is there any water to drink." So Moses and Aaron went from the presence of the assembly to the door of the tabernacle of meeting, and they fell on their faces. And the glory of the LORD appeared to them. Then the LORD spoke to Moses, saying, "Take the rod; you and your brother Aaron gather the congregation together. Speak to the rock before their eyes, and it will yield its water; thus you shall bring water for them out of the rock, and give drink to the congregation and their animals." So Moses took the rod from before the LORD as He commanded him. And Moses and Aaron gathered the assembly together before the rock; and he said to them, "Hear now, you rebels! Must we bring water for you out of this rock?" Then Moses lifted his hand and struck the rock twice with his rod; and water came out abundantly, and the congregation and their animals drank. Then the LORD spoke to Moses and Aaron, "Because you did not believe Me, to hallow Me in the eyes of the children of Israel, therefore you shall not bring this assembly into the land which I have given them." (Numbers 20:2-12)

These two events were critical in the leadership of Moses. They were both testing times for Moses. However, Moses saw them as the expression of the stubbornness of the people of God and failed to realize within the instructions lies his own test of leadership. He allowed the behaviors of the congregation to crowd his sense of reasoning as a result; his decisions were flawed. As Christian leaders, the attitude of certain members of your congregation can be unbecoming. Except for the Grace of God, you could have lost it.

The events at the Rocks were special events not for Moses and his congregation alone, but for us the new creation in Jesus Christ. They were foundation events pointing to the coming of Jesus Christ and his purpose as revealed by Apostle Paul.

> Moreover, brethren, I do not want you to be unaware that all our fathers were under the cloud, all passed through the sea, all were baptized into Moses in the cloud and in the sea, all ate the same spiritual food, and all drank the same spiritual drink, for they drank of that spiritual Rock that followed them, and that Rock was Christ. But with most of them God was not well pleased, for their bodies were scattered in the wilderness. (1st Corinthians 10:1-5)

Apostle Paul as seen above, revealed the Rock was the symbol of Jesus Christ. By the same token, the water was representative of the eternal water of life that Jesus Christ offers (John 4:10-14).

> Jesus answered and said to her, "If you knew the gift of God, and who it is who says to you, 'Give Me a drink,' you would have asked Him, and He would have given you living water." The woman said to Him, "Sir, You have nothing to draw with, and the well is deep.

> Where then do You get that living water? Are You greater than our father Jacob, who gave us the well, and drank from it himself, as well as his sons and his livestock?" Jesus answered and said to her, "Whoever drinks of this water will thirst again, but whoever drinks of the water that I shall give him will never thirst. But the water that I shall give him will become in him a fountain of water springing up into everlasting life." (John 4:10-14)

God instructing, Moses to strike the Rock at Horeb (Exodus 17:5-6) was the figurative depiction of crucifying Jesus Christ for the sins of humanity. This metaphoric expression becomes clearer when God instructed Moses to speak to the Rock at Kadesh (Numbers 20:8-11). This implies Jesus Christ haven been crucified, dead buried, and resurrected. It was no longer necessary to strike the Rock as that would mean crucifying the Son of God all over again and subjecting him to public disgrace (Hebrews 6:6). What is required was to; speak to the rock for the spiritual water of life to flow. By this event, God effectively established speaking as the Christian leader's instrument of change. Christian leaders are required to demonstrate the power in their tongue by speaking to a circumstance for a change. God spoke the world into being (Genesis 1:1-31). Jesus Christ controlled chaos by speaking (Mark 4:35-41). The books of Proverbs caution that the power of life and death in our tongue (Proverbs 18:21)

As the team leader, Moses disobedience sets a dangerous precedent for the church. Obeying basic sets of instructions ensures good coordination and team cohesion. As a spiritual leader, Moses had a responsibility to always act in faith on divine instruction. He also takes responsibility for the spiritual and physical well-being of himself and his congregation.

Perhaps, Moses was upset out of frustration and fatigue and as a result, he disobeyed God. Samson was another great leaders who out of frustration and fatigue let the enemy in. (Judges 16:16-19). How about Esau? Esau had been out in the field and was exhausted. He needed a refreshing but, went to the wrong source. As a result, he exchanged his destiny for a pot of stew (Genesis 25:29-34). How many times out of frustration in the ministry, have you gone to some close associates without consulting God and you ended up in a deeper mess.

Christian leaders must be aware that in the ministry, there are moments like those of Moses, Esau, and Samson where we are despaired, desperate, and might even want to quit.

God will not succumb to our limits because He has given us His strength. When you sense frustration and exhaustion as church leaders get a break (see Chapter 8 - self-care and stress management). Jesus Christ often goes to quiet places for prayers. Prayers are not always about asking, but, an opportunity to be ministered to. Apart from his early life, the Bible has no record of Moses personal life in the ministry, I am not sure he had one, his wife and two sons perhaps lived the best part of their lives with his father-in-law Jethro. But, when you examine the event and comments of Zipporah in the following verses;

> **And it came to pass by the way in the inn, that the LORD met him, and sought to kill him. Then Zipporah took a sharp stone, and cut**

> off the foreskin of her son, and cast it at his feet, and said, Surely a bloody husband art thou to me. So he let him go: then she said, A bloody husband thou art, because of the circumcision. (Exodus 4:24-26)

It looks like Moses didn't have a cohesive household. Perhaps, his wife was more decisive and apt. The ministry is not an excuse to neglect your spouse, children, and self-care.

Moses has no right to complain about his congregation because the congregation were not his, but, belong to God Almighty (Psalm 95:7; Psalm 100:3; Ephesians 5:23; Colossians 1:18). Most church leaders habitually complain about the overseer and perhaps the church boards as well as the congregation. Beloved quit this habit; it is a risky place to be. When, you, receive a specific set of instructions from God, your safest position is to obey. Thus, God held Moses accountable for his disobedience. The gravity of disobeying God is not measurable. For the singular momentary act of disobedience to God, Moses was not permitted to enter the Promised Land (Numbers. 20:12).

The Place of Revelation in Leadership

Other times, when Satan shows in your marriage or ministry, it takes the spirit of discernment to understand the unusual behavior in your spouse, child, or congregation is manipulation from Satan. Peter's revelation of Jesus Christ's identity was the single qualification that offered him the leadership position. It does behove Christian leaders to always seek God with matters of the church and eschew human wisdom. They need to understand and work with the mind of God.

> When Jesus came into the region of Caesarea Philippi, He asked His disciples, saying, "Who do men say that I, the Son of Man, am? "So, they said, "Some say John the Baptist, some Elijah, and others Jeremiah or one of the prophets. "He said to them, "But who do you say that I am? "Simon Peter answered and said, "You are the Christ, the Son of the living God. "Jesus answered and said to him, "Blessed are you, Simon Bar-Jonah, for flesh and blood has not revealed this to you, but My Father who is in heaven. And I also say to you that you are Peter, and on this rock I will build My church, and the gates of Hades shall not prevail against it. And I will give you the keys of the kingdom of heaven, and whatever you bind on earth will be bound in heaven, and whatever you loose on earth will be loosed in heaven." (Matthew 16:13-19).

Managing Church Crises

This leadership book culminates in obedience as the essential requirement of the Godly leaders. Having discussed spiritual leadership in depth here is how not to choose a spiritual leader to prevent crises in the church. Conceivably it also serves as an example of how spiritual leadership differs from circular leadership.

> Then the mother of Zebedee's sons came to Him with her sons, kneeling down and asking something from Him. And He said to her,

> "What do you wish?"
>
> She said to Him, "Grant that these two sons of mine may sit, one on Your right hand and the other on the left, in Your kingdom."
>
> But Jesus answered and said, "You do not know what you ask. Are you able to drink the cup that I am about to drink, and be baptized with the baptism that I am baptized with?"
>
> They said to Him, "We are able."
>
> So He said to them, "You will indeed drink My cup, and be baptized with the baptism that I am baptized with; but to sit on My right hand and on My left is not Mine to give, but it is for those for whom it is prepared by My Father."
>
> And when the ten heard it, they were greatly displeased with the two brothers. But Jesus called them to Himself and said, "You know that the rulers of the Gentiles lord it over them, and those who are great exercise authority over them. Yet it shall not be so among you; but whoever desires to become great among you, let him be your servant. And whoever desires to be first among you, let him be your slave just as the Son of Man did not come to be served, but to serve, and to give His life a ransom for many." (Matthew 20:20-28 - NKJV)

As would be expected, the request of this mother for her sons resulted in acrimony amongst Jesus Christ leadership team. As the remaining ten were upset. However, the character of the mother in these scriptures highlights the failure of our contemporary leadership approaches. Church leadership today is a family affair. The church founder and, immediate members of his or her family occupies the core and most sensitive leadership positions. The next set of leaders is friends of the founder and their families. So, this mother wanted her two sons to fill the two positions of Jesus Christ deputies as we see in our churches today. Incidentally, her two sons were already members of Jesus Christ's inner team (Matthew 10:2-4).

Jesus Christ resolved the conflict by first inviting them and reminding them of the unique nature of their leadership. Their leadership is not like the circular style of leadership Jesus Christ explained to them. The center truth from the response of Jesus Christ is that spiritual leadership is essentially God's choice, and it is about serving Him through serving others. Serving God through serving others as established in Jesus Christ's teachings (Matthew 7:21-23) is a demonstration of agape love. God's love is expressed by the church leadership in helping the congregation grow and matures in God.

This also reveals delegation of task and responsibilities as one of the areas in church and ministry that could be considered a stressor for the minister. Certain members of the congregation want to occupy the juicy offices in the church. This has resulted in serious conflicts among the brethren in the church that requires crises management. Crises management in the church is a sensitive issue that draws on the wisdom of the church elders and leaders in fruitful harmony. Like conflicts in the marriage, anything can result in a crisis in the ministry.

In conclusion, , church crises can be internal or external. Currently, the coronavirus is the most recent external crisis the church has faced in recent times. It has redefined the mode and medium of church services and created an unprecedented disruption in our social and family coexistence. Like the medical personnel, church leaders are supposed to play a leading role, in reassuring the populace with scriptural evidence even as they engage and adjust to life with and after coronavirus. But, how ready are you as a Christian leader?

About the Author

Senior Pastor Teresa McCurry is an ordained minister of the Gospel of Jesus Christ. She co-labors with her husband, Apostle Gregory McCurry, of New Beginning Ministries (NBM) doing the work of the Lord as a ministry team.

> **"We introduce a Real God, to Real
> people with Real issues"**

Pastor Tee was called to ministry in 2010 under the leadership of Apostle Leon and Pastor Margie Nelson. She has traveled extensively, educating and inspiring others with her unique approach of conveying information. She has a heart for doing missions work around the world. She was sent into the Office of a Prophet and consecrated in 2018.

This was the beginning of a great and powerful deliverance move of God in her life to reach the hurting and lost. God anointed Pastor Tee with spiritual eyesight and ability to speak into people's lives and immediately deliverance takes place to bring forth healing to broken-hearted souls, to proclaim liberty to the captives and set their hearts completely free.

Pastor Tee is dedicated to helping people who seek to make a positive change.

Her marketplace ministry extends beyond the walls of the church. She is a Beauty Entrepreneur, Inspirational Speaker, International Bible Teacher and International Bestselling Author: she has been a licensed cosmetologist with over 30 years of beauty industry experience. She holds a Bachelor's degree in Applied Business Administration. Teresa's passion for the beauty industry standards are displayed in the excellence with which she leads by example, educating, serving, and beautifying clients while inspiring them to reach their God-given purpose.

Teresa's Discipleship is personal and unscripted. She is prophetic in nature and lead by the Holy Spirit. What she offers is leadership training that is personalized to each of her Disciples' unique situations and needs. She works with a limited number of clients each year, and she works with them in a few different ways: Personal Discipleship, Signature Group Discipleship Coaching, and PTU ~ Pastor Tee University *(coming Soon)*.

She is currently known as Super Tee; she chairs Christian Networking Entrepreneurs "CNE" and NBM Community

Outreach. Through CNE we encourage creative thinking, inspire meaningful dialogue and promote personal and business development through fellowship that will spotlight and support Christian businesses.

Super Tee is the founder of the MCS~Fund whose sole mission is to generate unrestricted funds for Sickle Cell Anemia affected individuals. Through Supportive Services & Advocacy, serving the needs of people plagued by this disease is not only a mission but a passion.

Pastor Tee's "honors and awards": she received an honorary doctorate in Humanitarian for having over 20 years of volunteer service to the Sickle cell community from the Global International Alliance By the Authority of the International Association of Christian Counselors.

Pastor Tee also serves on the Board of Directors at Detroit Shoreway Community Development Organization (DSCDO), as Board Secretary and Institutional Representative.

Dr. Juanita Foster

A Doctor of Leadership who loves teaching, and arts and crafts!

As the owner of Educate Motivate Elevate Consulting, LLC, I help, business leaders and teams gain confidence, and cohesiveness so them and their organization experience profitable growth.

I do this by offering private consulting services to leaders who want to build their confidence and reach their personal and professional goal.

Also, I conduct interactive and engaging workshops. Juanita is known as a training workshop leader who is passionate, and engaging that captivates various audiences.

Juanita's workshop can be customized to meet the needs and objectives of any audience (individuals, organizations or teams).

My accomplishments include:

- Ed. D. in Organizational Leadership
- MS in Organizational Leadership
- BS in Business Management
- Certified Staff Development Trainer
- Certified Life Coach
- Certified Nursing Assistant
- International Speaker
- International Amazon Best Selling Author
- Written State of Delaware Approved Curriculum for Early Childhood Education
- Successful Business Owner
- 15 + years working for Fortune 500 Company

www.ingramcontent.com/pod-product-compliance
Lightning Source LLC
Chambersburg PA
CBHW030859170426
43193CB00009BA/677